Not Just A Sound

Not
Just A Sound
The Story of
WLW

⊂×⊃×⊂×⊃×⊂

By Dick Perry

×××

PRENTICE-HALL, INC.
Englewood Cliffs, N. J.

Acknowledgments:
Material from Mary Wood's columns reprinted by permission, Cincinnati
    Post and Times-Star.
Quotes from thesis by Lawrence Wilson Lichty copyright © 1964.
    Reprinted by permission.
Extracts from *Here's Bob* by Bob Braun copyright © 1969 by
    Bob Braun. Reprinted by permission of Doubleday & Company, Inc.
Quotes from *Paul Baby* reprinted by permission of The World Pub-
    lishing Company from *Paul Baby* by Paul Dixon. An NAL book.
    Copyright © 1968 by The New American Library, Inc.
Quotes from *Ladies' Home Journal* © 1960 Downes Publishing, Inc.
    Reprinted by special permission of *Ladies' Home Journal.*
Extracts from "Ruth Lyons/VIP Coming Up" reprinted by special per-
    mission of *American Home Magazine* © 1958 Downe Publishing, Inc.
Extracts from "The Loudest Voice in the World," by Arthur W. Baum,
    reprinted by permission of *The Saturday Evening Post* © 1944 Curtis
    Publishing Co.
Extracts from "The Lady Lays Down the Law," by James Maxwell, reprinted
    by permission of *The Saturday Evening Post* © 1957 Curtis Publishing Co.

Books by Dick Perry
Raymond and Me That Summer
The Roundhouse, Paradise, and Mr. Pickering
Vas You Ever in Zinzinnati?
One Way To Write Your Novel
Ohio, A Personal Portrait of the 17th State
The Jesse Stuart Conversations
Not Just A Sound: The Story of WLW
Plays by Dick Perry
Go From Me
The Briefcase Bohemian of the 7:54
Forever The Wild, Sweet Voice of Lovers
There'll Never Be Another Bongo
Who'll Teach My Baby Razor-Blades?
What It Was, Was Oxford?

WLW is not just a sound;
it is a vital part of the community
in which that sound is heard

In 1972, WLW and I are fifty years old. We were both born in Cincinnati. But there the comparison stops. WLW remains young. I am growing old. While I have three offspring (two handsome lads and one beautiful girl) WLW has eleven—in the form of five television stations (WLWT, Cincinnati; WLWD, Dayton; WLWC, Columbus; WLWI, Indianapolis, and WOAI-TV, San Antonio), and six radio stations (WRTH, Wood River, Illinois; WOAI, San Antonio; WWDC and WWDC-FM, Washington, D.C., and KYA and KOIT, San Francisco. WLW also has had more shortwave stations then I would care to list. At the beginning, though, I had more lung power than WLW Radio had broadcast power. I could be heard three houses away; sometimes WLW couldn't. And *I* did not have to stop bawling once every hour so ships in distress on the high seas could be heard. WLW did. But soon WLW was outshouting me. Once when it broadcast experimentally with 500,000 watts it outshouted every commercial broadcasting station in the United States. Its signal strength was so powerful you didn't need a radio receiver to hear it. Some say the station came in on the milking machines near the Mason, Ohio, transmitter. Others claim WLW came in on the barbed wire fences. All I know is, in Sedamsville where I lived, WLW always came in real good. WLW and I grew up together.

Each of us is of a *certain* moment in broadcast history. Each of us is, in some wonderful way, the product of the broadcasting that was heaped upon us in our childhood. By broadcasting, I mean both radio *and* television. WLW has always been there, first with radio and then, the year I got married to Jean, married to television. For those keeping a scorecard, note that the year was 1948. My children, for example, grew up in the television era of Howdy Doody, Pinky Lee, Wyatt Earp, the Mouseketeers, and Davy Crockett. Another generation came of age during Batman. Another generation, though it frightens me to contemplate it, is coming up via *Dark Shadows*. Well, no matter. Just as the present generation, in love with *Dark Shadows* and amiable neck-bites, looks down with scorn on those who thought they knew for sure that Mickey Mouse really loved them, so does the Mickey Mouse generation look down upon us—across that long reach of time —because we happened to think that Jack Armstrong *was* the real All-American Boy. Jim Ameche, Don's brother, was the first to play that role on radio and only the other day I glimpsed him on the tube, selling record albums, and he has sure changed a lot. I sensed with a finality that only one approaching fifty can sense, that times have changed.

But this will be about WLW, now and then. The WLW of *my* childhood is not the WLW of today and neither am

I. I mean, who remembers *Harry Horlick's A&P Gypsies; Al Pearce and His Gang* ("Nobody home, I hope, I hope, I hope"), *The Aldrich Family* with Ezra Stone; *The Baby Snooks Show* with Fanny Brice; Ben Bernie, Bob Burns, *Buck Rogers, Bulldog Drummond, Chandu the Magician,* and *The Lady Next Door?* Only we who are approaching the fifty mark do and we would rather not be reminded of it, if you don't mind. Still, WLW radio then was a beautiful thing. It is now, I suppose, but styles in beauty change. *Moon River* has sloshed its way to the sea and is gone, gone forever. WLW is fresh out of silver ribbon to wind up the cares of night. Peter Grant won't recite love poems at my wife no more. But oh, back then radio was sweet. It was the radio many of us grew up with, wasn't it? But would I listen again to Pa and Ma McCormick? Would I listen again to *Ma Perkins?* Would I again attend the *Church by the Side of the Road* or a concert by the Armco Band? I must be honest and say no. That was yesterday's radio. Yesterday's radio, for all its wonderful remembering, is a good place to visit but I wouldn't want to live there. By today's standards, yesterday's broadcasts are corny. Sorry to say it, but there you are. Yet we can look at them again with fond memories, can't we? We can return again to the days of Smoke Dreams and when that old Rhinelander was spinning yarns of things that happened during Canal Days, can't we? And, by the same token, we can look at broadcasting of only yesterday at WLW, when television first began and wrestlers were a way of television life, can't we? And can't we also look at what fifty years of programming have wrought: from Mr. Crosley *himself* spinning records on a windup Victrola into a morning glory horn of a microphone to Mr. Dixon gazing with devilish fondness at the knees of the ladies who attend his morning show?

All of this is WLW, isn't it?

The question is, how did it all begin? For each of us it began when we ourselves began to listen or to watch. For most of us, WLW began before any of us were able to attend. While I waited around awhile in diapers learning to talk, WLW—born the same year—was talking a blue streak. By the time I had mastered the art of communication, WLW was so far down the road ahead of me that to catch up with it was impossible. So here I sit, becalmed, looking back to see where WLW has been, looking about to see where it is, and now and then gazing into a crystal ball that has never worked before to see where—if possible —WLW is going.

The book is casually divided into two sections. The first part carries us, in ten year swaths of time, through the twenties, thirties, forties, and into the fifties. Then we get so involved in television personalities the book's organization falls apart. At that point, we back off and take a running leap at four key personalities in depth (Ruth Lyons, Bob Braun, Paul Dixon, Phil Donahue) because their stories *are* the stories of Avco Broadcasting's television operation. In other words, the first part of the book will wander down memory lane and the second part of the book will take a closer look at some of the people who made and are still making Avco Broadcasting the force that it is.

If Cincinnati things—and its broadcasting personalities —are lost upon you, let me make here a fast and casual explanation of several items. Ruth Lyons, for twenty-five years, first on radio, then on the tube, can be considered the Arthur Godfrey of WLW-land. There will be those who question this. Some say her influence was greater than Godfrey's ever was. She ran a gabby talk show and ran it well. Paul Dixon, whom you will meet, started as a radio disc jockey and now himself runs another gabby show. When he says to buy something, the viewers do. Bob Braun, who took over when Ruth Lyons retired, is a dimpled darling who has charm that won't quit; you will like him as you will like Dixon. Phil Donahue has another kind of show—a thoughtful one that appeals to the intellect of the housewives; each day a different guest on the hot seat. You will hear also of *Moon River*, *not* the song but the program of dreamy organ music, dreamy poetry, and dreamy moods which WLW used to transmit late each night to put old people to sleep and to get lovers on with the business at hand. Peter Grant's golden voice read much of the poetry. Now retired, he was—and still is—the dean of all announcers, network and local. He came to WLW in the thirties and just recently retired. All these people came along later, though. I note them here so the strangers among us will be able to tell the players apart.

First there was Powel Crosley, Jr. He started the station. There are those historians who suggest that Mr. Crosley changed the spelling of his first name from *Powell* to *Powel* because the one-l'd name worked better insofar as numerology was concerned. There are those historians who differ. These say that records show he always spelled his first name with one *l*. To look up his birth record at the Hamilton County Courthouse in Cincinnati is impossible. No record exists there. But as for the man himself, he has been described as a diverse person. They say he was diverse in moods and dreams as well. Sometimes he has been described as "warm and homespun." Also, they say, he would fly into a rage now and then. Some employees described him as aloof. Another said, "He was one of the boys." Other adjectives attached to him are "warm, intelligent, self-effacing, and competent." Though he liked to mingle with the boys, as some have said, others have said that the only time they ever saw him was on the elevator. What you thought of him, it seems, depends on who you were and what you were doing at the time.

His folks came from Warren County near Lebanon, Ohio, where now the Golden Lamb Inn is and it was there then, too. He was born September 18, 1886—eighty-seven years to the day before Jean and I were married. His father had come to Cincinnati where he divided his time between the practice of law and real estate. Two years after the Hamilton County Courthouse was burned in Cincinnati, Mr. Powel Crosley, Jr., came into the world. The year he was born, 1886, Dan McCaffrey fought John L. Sullivan in Cincinnati's Chester Park. To make our history complete, he was born the year the Art Museum opened in Eden Park. When he was about seven, his parents moved from Kemper Lane to College Hill. What kind of world was his childhood? Well, in Cincinnati then more than five thousand steamboats arrived and departed from the waterfront. And the city itself was building more than half the carriages used in the United States. As for school, he attended the public school in College Hill and the Ohio Military Institute located in the same neighborhood. But he was forever the dreamer and thinker and doer.

Said one magazine article in a quote from him, "When I was twelve years old I decided it was about time for me to take a swing at the world. At the time, the automobile was the scientific but unpredictable wonder of the day,

[6]

but to me its future was assured. So I was determined to build one. Rather short on capital at the moment, I borrowed eight dollars from my younger brother, Lewis, and with his help I concocted a four-wheeled wagon, powered it with an electric motor and battery, and displayed it to my father as my 'invention.' He looked at it with the gloomiest eyes. In fact, he thought so little of my contraption that he offered me ten dollars if it would work. After the test—my 'automobile' had traversed the whole block— I accepted the ten dollars, paid Lewis his eight, plus a dollar as his share of the profit, and gloatingly pocketed my dollar, convinced that I had embarked on a great industrial career in the new mechanical age."

Stories about the car he *did* put out to market are legion—we should get to some of them in this book— but the one that sticks in my mind is the one involved in advertising the car. Ralph Jones was the advertising agency that handled the account of the Crosley car, the forerunner of the Volkswagen which later captured the hearts —and the pocketbooks—of the American public. The poor lad whose job it was to write the ads for the Crosley car was beside himself with frustration. He and everyone in the agency wanted Mr. Crosley to run big full-page ads telling of the wonder of the gadget, but Crosley was firm.

"It is a *small* car," he said. "Therefore we will run *small* ads for it."

Now the Crosley car is no more. A few still toot along the highways, but not many. They are remnants of a dream that bore fruit before its time.

As for formal education, Powel Crosley attended the University of Cincinnati. First he studied engineering. Then, because his father asked him to, he switched to

[7]

law college. But he was too restless to stick with either. His love was still automobiles. In 1906, to get closer to his love, he quit college to get a job as a chauffeur so he could have the pleasure of driving one. Also, he held other jobs. He sold bonds. He was a telephone lineman. In 1907, when he turned twenty-one, he borrowed $10,000 to build his first car, one that he himself had designed. It was called the "Marathon Six." It had, as you might have guessed, six cylinders. He designed it to sell for around $1,700—several hundred dollars less than dealers were then asking for two- and three-cylinder cars. But time was not in his favor. In 1907, there was a panic. Dollars were scarce. The new company, hardly in business, went out of business fast. He put the dream away—for a while. But he still hung around cars a lot.

He broke his arm cranking a car that he had entered in the Indianapolis 500. He had to drop from the race. He moved from city to city and from job to job—mostly in Indiana and Michigan and mostly in jobs connected with automobiles—until 1911. He came back to start still another company, selling cycle cars, but though they were the rage, no one seemed to be buying lots of them, so he let his new company go the way of all flesh. He got a job writing advertising copy. On the side, however, the love for autos refused to die. He developed a plan to advertise a product called the "Gastronic." It was, they say, the first gasoline fortifier. The product's owner, in the automobile accessory business, wanted to know if Crosley had any more ideas to peddle to automobile owners. And also he asked Crosley, "Can you figure out some way we can sell reliners made from old tires?"

Crosley could. He came up with the mail-order plan to

offer them, via agents, as "Insyde Tires." With a $500 advance, the company with the high-sounding name was launched. It was called the American Automobile Accessories Company which might not impress you terribly much, but follow the bouncing ball because that was the start of WLW, *Moon River*, Peter Grant, and *Midwestern Hayride*. Crosley, though involved with the new company, had learned his lesson. He still continued to do advertising jobs on the side, moonlighting to bring in the dollars. Also note that this business of selling auto by-products to car owners almost ended before it began because back then the world of the car owner was different. At the first hint of winter in the Ohio Valley, the first flake of snow or cold weather, the car owners tucked their cars away till spring. No one—or at least only the very brave—drove. But Crosley stuck with his dream: if he couldn't sell cars, he could at least sell pieces of them to car owners.

One of the items he created was patriotic and profitable. World War I was going on then. He designed and sold a flag-holder that fit on the radiator cap. Records suggest that he sold thousands and thousands of them. Also, he designed and built an *anti-draft* shield, not for the would-be draft dodgers but for Model T Fords. This shield could be placed above the windshield itself to eliminate drafts. He also invented a thing called "The Litl Shofur" which was another help for those struggling along the bumpy roads in their Model T Fords. This was a device which returned the car to a straight line after the driver had been jolted silly by a rock in the road.

"The success of relatively unimportant and inexpensive products," recalled Mr. Crosley later, "convinced me that I should appeal to the masses rather than the classes, and

[9]

by serving them—at the lowest possible cost to consumer —I would profit the most."

Thus, the company which started out as the American Automobile Accessories Company soon found itself making a host of other things. Some of them were not related to automobiles at all. For instance, his company made phonograph cabinets. It also made canoes. And, later on, after buying out a printing establishment, it made all of its own advertising, too. By 1921—the year before WLW came on the radio—the company was doing a million-dollar business and making a profit of ten percent. *I Love Lucy* might not have been invented yet, but for a man in business those were—indeed—the good old days.

Then came radio.

The twenties, in which radio saw the light—or noise— of day, were in recollection, sweet and beguiling years. Anyone for Memory Lane? The decade of the twenties which saw the start of radio for real was a street filled with tin Lizzies, skirts far below the knees, a trolley line for 'most every neighborhood, Sacco and Vanzetti, Lucky Lindy, patent-leather hair, Barney Google, Clara Bow, and coast-to-coast by train in forty-eight hours. The twenties meant the syncopated sound instead of the rock we hear today. We played records—breakable seventy-eights—that bore the labels of Victor, Harmony, Gennett, Paramount, Black Swan, and Columbia. We heard, through the morning glory horn, the Club Wigwam Orchestra play *Alabamy Bound;* Fletcher Henderson's *Swamp Blues;* Baby Bonnie's *Home Sweet Home Blues;* and Ozie Ware do the *Hit Me in the Nose Again Blues.* In the twenties we entered the years that would bring us Billy Jones and Ernie Hare, Jessica Dragonette, Rudy Vallee, and the Masked Tenor of Good-

[10]

rich (he turned out to be "little known Joe White"). It was the moment of ornate movie palaces. It was when everyone said, "Quick, Henry, the Flit!" It was the decade when they laughed when you sat down to the piano, when you were a ninety-seven pound weakling, and Wall Street—at the beginning—started out nice. Babe Ruth made a movie called *The Babe Comes Home*. Jack Dempsey spoke French—they say—in his movie *So This Is Paris*. And, of course, the Noble Experiment was the Noble Experiment —or who's got the bathtub gin? The twenties represented the season of Al Capone, Cincinnati's George Remus, and George "Bugs" Moran who was going pretty good until the St. Valentine's Day Massacre in that garage in Chicago. It was the moment of Edna St. Vincent Millay who wrote:

> My candle burns at both ends;
> It will not last the night;
> But, ah, my foes, and oh, my friends—
> It gives a lovely light! *

It was the moment of Langston Hughes who wrote:

> We cry among the skyscrapers
> As our ancestors
> Cried among the palms in Africa
> Because we are alone,
> It is night,
> And we're afraid.**

It was the time of Eugene O'Neill and of *Main Street* by Sinclair Lewis. Add Will Rogers to the decade. And add Calvin Coolidge. Add Jimmy Walker. And Rudolph Valen-

---

[11]

tino. It was the moment in time when Douglas Fairbanks —the first of them—was young. If you didn't sit on flag-poles you got your kicks from Mah-Jongg. Or, later in the decade, danced yourself to exhaustion in a marathon. Or, while driving, you read the resident poet at work in the hire of Burma Shave. The world back then seemed ready for anything. What it got was radio.

Some people went into the radio business headfirst. Crosley seemed to back into it, finding himself in the middle of the new industry almost by accident. This makes sense, though. Automobiles were his first love. They were his second, third, fourth, and fifth love, too. Radio, actually, was rather far down on the list if it had been on his list at all. How *did* he get into the radio business? Well, he tells it best himself: "One day my son came home with a glow-ing description of a new wireless outfit." The son, Powel III, begged his father to buy one for him. The father said sure, thinking the gadget was little more than a toy, but when he and his son went shopping the next day for one of the "wireless gadgets" Powel Crosley, Jr., was somewhat shocked. No matter how many stores they shopped, the lowest-priced "wireless" still cost more than $100. So the father did the next best thing. Rather than spend $100, he spent 25¢ for a book called the *ABC's of Radio*. Said the father:

"I read the book and it intrigued me. A couple of days later I went back to the shop and asked if I could buy the parts separately and assemble the radio myself. For be-tween $20 and $25 I returned home with headphones, a tuning coil, a crystal detector, a condenser, and other mysti-fying gadgets."

He managed to put them all together and received Pittsburgh! He was properly intrigued. He hurried back to the shop and had them build him a set that cost $200. In the summer of 1921 he ordered, in addition, a 20-watt transmitter and started sending recorded music out over the air. He said, "Before I knew it, I had virtually forgotten my regular business in the interest of radio."

But something bothered him. He recalled, "I wondered how other men on salaries as small as mine managed to buy radio sets at the prices advertised? I knew that the expensive equipment I had been shown was out of the question for them. I also knew that many men lacked the mechanical knowledge—or desire—to build their own sets. I was confident that the radio set was not going to be a rich man's toy and that it had to be within the reach of everyone."

Besides, he was still the businessman. His phonograph business was declining. He wanted something to keep his plant in full operation. Why not, he decided, make radio receiving sets? He hired two young engineers from the University of Cincinnati and turned the project over to them. One was Dorman Israel who later became chairman of Emerson Radio and Phonograph. Mr. Israel designed a radio receiving set that worked and that could, better yet, be produced inexpensively. It was a simple crystal receiver. It was called "The Harko." Mr. Crosley had a way with names, didn't he? Anyway, it sold for $20 at first. Later it sold for $9, but don't get too upset. By the time you bought headphones to go with it so you could hear Pittsburgh and by the time you bought the antenna, you had spent about $15. The Harko was sold during the Christmas season of 1921. It was a roaring success. It was such a success that Mr. Crosley got so busy making Harkos that he stopped—for a moment—dreaming about making automobiles. Soon his phonograph plant was turning out Harkos so fast it had no time to turn out phonograph cabinets at all. He was in the business of selling radio receivers for real.

Since he sold radios, he wanted his customers to hear something when they bought them. The next step is logical. He got permission from the government to put a radio station on the air. The station, given the call letters WLW, went on the air in March, 1922. Radio, though new, was not *that* new. By the summer of 1920, nearly two years before WLW came on the air, there were many radio stations in the United States, most of them rather freak operations that wandered, like thoughtless children, from one dial position to another. As early as 1912, Dr. Frank Conrad had been tinkering with the idea of "wireless." Actually even before that, in 1909, in San Jose, California, Charles David Herrold had operated a radio broadcasting station on a more or less scheduled basis. 1917 had found the University of Wisconsin experimenting. So which was the first station ever to go on the air? David Sarnoff said, "I believe that the answer . . . is lost beyond recall in the early unrecorded days of broadcasting." The start of broadcasting is said by many to be November 2, 1920, which was the night KDKA in Pittsburgh aired the election returns which found Warren G. Harding elected President. The same night the station also played music—from phonograph records. What do the Washington records show on who is first? Well, September 15, 1921, the Department of Commerce, then handling radio matters, issued a regular broadcast license to WBZ, then of Springfield, but later Boston. This is supposed to be the first license recorded, but by no means was WBZ first on the air. Anybody who could put together a transmitter got on the air, legally or otherwise.

It can be safely said that WLW was among the first stations on the air. In January, 1922, only twenty-eight stations were officially broadcasting; a month later eight more had been added to the roster to bring the total to thirty-six. By March, sixty-five stations were on the air. So we can say that WLW-Radio is one of the first sixty-five stations in the country. Had Crosley waited a month, he would have found himself in a crowd. By the end of April, 1922, there were 133 stations broadcasting. By the end of December, there were 570. Of the 570 that went on the air the year WLW did, about 140 are still operating. Who owned those 570 stations? Just about everybody and his brother. Some were owned by newspapers, educational institutions, churches, banks, department stores, YMCA's, government agencies, railroads, parks, theaters, and automobile dealers. One, according to Lawrence Wilson Lichty (who wrote an exhaustive thesis on the subject) was even owned by a laundry!

To make matters interesting, all the radio stations were on one of two frequencies. If they weren't at the 485 spot on your dial, telling you about the weather and how the hog prices were, they were to be found at 360 on your dial, entertaining you with music, sermons, and whatever news items the broadcaster could muster. By the fall of 1922, however, the stations were allowed to spread out a little to other places on the dial, but there were still moments of broadcast confusion. The confusion, though, wasn't too rampant. None of the stations broadcast full time as most do today.

The *first* studios of WLW were in Powel Crosley, Jr.'s, home in College Hill. The first transmitter was a 20-watt job that contained four five-watt tubes and had been built by the Standard Precision Instrument Company. This, though, was when WLW *wasn't* WLW. It had been authorized as a "special land station" by the Department of Commerce sometime during the summer of 1921, the call letters being 8XAA. WLW became WLW in March, 1922, if that helps. Some say the original call letters were 8CR, and those of you who are fond of old call letters, as I am, are probably wondering where 8CR vanished. Well, the only record of 8CR's existence seems to be in the news releases that Crosley, Jr., himself wrote. He said 8CR was the forerunner of WLW. The Department of Commerce, then licensing stations, has no record of it; the department says his first station was the aforementioned 8XAA. Shall we leave that discussion to the ages?

When WLW was officially authorized, it was allowed 50 watts of power and broadcast at the 360 spot on the dial, unless you were without a dial and fiddling with a cat-whisker at the time. In September, 1922, Crosley moved his radio station from his home to his new manufacturing plant in the Mill Creek Valley. The studio—heavily cur-tained—contained the transmitter. According to old-timers, when summer came, the transmitter got warm, and the studio became an oven. The first WLW microphone was a huge morning glory horn, eight feet long, and you shouted into the big end of it which was three feet across. Actually, you didn't shout into it, you stuck your head halfway down into it to be heard. Phonograph music was played by putting the morning glory horn of the phonograph player against the morning glory horn that was the microphone.

Those must have been the good old days. The Mill Creek Valley, where the studio was, is a heavily industrial valley lined with many railroad tracks. Trains were always shrieking steam whistle shrieks at crossings and at whatever struck their fancy. It is said that the train whistles could be heard in the studio and over the air waves by those brave souls cranked into radioland. It is also said the train noises at times became so loud that the station waited until the noisy train passed before continuing with its programming.

Because a radio station in Atlanta advertised itself as "The Voice of the South," a Kansas City station advertised itself as being the "Heart of the West," and one in Davenport, Iowa, advertised itself as "Where the West Begins" WLW, by the autumn of 1922, began calling itself the broadcasting station "for the Queen City of the West." Chances are, when you heard the announcer say it, you might have been listening to Powel Crosley, Jr., himself. For you who think *soul* is modern, note that in its very early years WLW used to identify itself with the announcer saying:

"This is WLW . . . The Station with a Soul."

Although Peter Grant seems such a fixture one assumes he predates Mr. Crosley at the WLW microphones, this is not so. When Crosley operated the station from his home, it was Crosley himself and, at times, Russell Blair, who stuck their heads deep into the morning glory horn microphones to tell which station was which. After the station moved to the factory, Robert Cooper and Robert Stayman also worked as WLW staff members—part-time, that is. Their full-time chores were with the manufacturing company Crosley ran. The usual program that WLW featured in those early days—and about the only program—was Powel Crosley, Jr., who, when not shouting call letters into the microphone, was playing "Song of India" on the phonograph player. Then he would shout into the microphone, asking if anyone out there had heard him. Then he would play "Song of India" again.

The first real program, they say, was when from the new —and hot—studios, Crosley had Giacinto Gorno sing an aria while his brother Romeo Gorno accompanied him on the piano and William Morgan Knox accompanied him on the violin. Just as the singer started, and really got going good, up Mill Creek Valley came a Baltimore & Ohio freight, its whistle whistling steamy counter-shrieks, and so everybody did the only thing that could be done.

They stopped, waited till the train passed, and started all over again.

What it was, was radio.

I_F Powel Crosley, Jr., can be called the father of WLW—
and he can—then Fred Smith can be called its midwife.
Said Mr. Crosley of Fred Smith whom he hired August,
1922:

"Fred came into my office one morning, rather apolo-
getically. He said he had nothing to sell to me, but wanted
to make some suggestions because he was so much interested in broadcasting. It seems that he had returned from
abroad shortly before then, where he had been for some
eight years. So I sounded him out—I do not know whether
or not he realized it at the time—but I made up my mind
that Fred would do a wonderful job of handling our broadcast work. I asked him how he would like to do it. He said
that the idea was entirely new to him, but that he could
think of nothing he would prefer to do. I talked to him a
few more minutes and asked him how soon he could start
. . . I finally succeeded in getting him to take off his hat

and coat and execute his plans before he went out of the office."

Fred Smith, just like that, became the first director of WLW. And, in addition, he became one of WLW's first announcers who had ladies out there in radioland fall in love with his voice. They were always writing him letters. If you question this, ask your grandmother how she felt about Fred Smith when each evening he signed on the station with his melodious "*Hello, hello, good evening. . .*"

Of course, WLW wasn't on the air every evening. In those days it shared time with other stations. The ladies who tuned in Fred Smith found that in December, 1922, they had to stay up later to do it. That was the month Crosley decided to sign WLW on at ten instead of at eight each Thursday. Why? To give the local listeners a chance to see what distant stations they could pull in. Sometimes, as you sat listening at one point on the dial, you heard a station drift by. This happened because several of the stations (*not* WLW, thank goodness!) operated with such makeshift equipment the station itself tended to drift casually about. In those days the trouble wasn't always in your receiving set. A lot of times it was in the station's transmitter! Also, Mr. Crosley was always seeking more and more power for his transmitter. Why? Because he was in the business of selling radio receivers at prices the man-on-the-street could afford which meant these early receivers worked but they were not the most sophisticated of sets like the higher-priced ones. Mr. Crosley reasoned with good sense that the more powerful WLW was, the better the station could be heard on the sets that working-men could afford.

In these less complicated days when we tune in usually

only the local channel on television, few of us viewers are interested in "distance." If, say, I am sitting watching the tube and seeing Paul Dixon do whatever he does (and I've yet to figure that out!) I am probably watching him over WLWT out of Cincinnati. I have little desire to see if my set and my antenna are good enough to pull Paul Dixon in from WLWC in Columbus. Why should I? Dixon is Dixon wherever you find him on the tube. Why settle for a fuzzy distant picture when a local one—sharp and bright and beautiful—is mine for the asking? But back in the early days of radio, part of the fun was seeing how many stations you could hear. If the man next door got Kansas City last night and you didn't, chances are you went around brooding for several days. Back then the listener was not interested in program quality. He was interested in seeing how many stations he could bring in. Simple as that.

When WLW first went on the air in March, 1922, letters came from as far away as Colorado, Maine, Michigan, Wisconsin, Connecticut, and Dent, Ohio. The inaugural broadcast was a stem-winder. Although the station had been officially broadcasting since March 2, the Grand Opening did not come about until March 23. That was when the station advertised locally that it was beginning a "regular broadcasting program schedule of news, lectures, information, and music." Cincinnati Mayor George P. Carrel said nice words about the venture on the inaugural program, the Capitol Theater jazz unit played, so did the Duo-Art reproducing piano. Miss Rose Boden sang. So did Mr. Oscar Colkers. No train passed to mar the event. The broadcast was heard not only in the homes but on Government Square in downtown Cincinnati where it was poured out over great speakers. The program, however, was not a non-

[21]

stop gala event. WLW stopped now and then to catch its breath. The program, supposed to start at 7:15 P.M., started at 7:30 P.M. and went off the air for intermission at nine. Said the *Cincinnati Enquirer*, the singers were broadcast with "clarity of tone." The mayor spoke about taxes as mayors are inclined to do.

The staff at WLW was forever trying to see how far WLW actually reached. In November, 1922, a contest was held. A book was awarded to the best letter from an adult and a child who said things about the WLW programs. One winner lived in Vallejo, California. In January, 1923, WLW offered a free box of candy to the first one from each state to send in a telegram. Entries were received from forty-two states! Three provinces of Canada answered as well as listeners from the District of Columbia. At the time, WLW broadcast with only 100 watts of power.

Powel Crosley, Jr., sent a copy of *The Crosley Radio Weekly* to whoever asked for it. He got requests from Maine to California with Cuba, Mexico, Panama, and the West Indies tossed in for good measure. In 1923, the publication went to more than twenty-five thousand listeners each week —everywhere. Also, WLW started its own fan club called "The Lightning Bugs." To join cost nothing. But members were required to "live the life of lightning bugs, coming forth at nightfall, or in time to hear the radio concerts over WLW." The club had ten thousand members. Each member had a special "lightning bug" pin.

What kind of programs did that early WLW toss out at its lightning bugs? Lots and lots of singers, to be sure, in singles or in groups. Lots of piano players. Lots of organ players. Now and then a boy soprano would come along to jar your nerves, or if he didn't, the man playing the musical saw did. The daytime programs were the products of the WLW employees. The nighttime programs were the products of anyone who happened to stray into the studio. One of the *first* programs to be broadcast on a regular basis in 1922 was—of all things!—the Central Parkway YMCA Swimming Instructor, Stanley Brauninger, giving swimming lessons. The series ran eight weeks, Wednesday evenings at eight. On Fridays, at 1:30 P.M., J. F. Roach broadcast guitar lessons. When Christmas came that year, Professor B. C. Van Wye of the University of Cincinnati read Dickens' *A Christmas Carol*. Actually, he read it the day after Christmas because on Christmas Day WLW was not scheduled to be on the air, but it was the thought that counted.

Also, there was drama—of a sort. They say that WLW was one of the first radio stations to tinker with drama, the first station actually being Schenectady's WGY which broadcast Eugene Walter's *The Wolf* August 3, 1922. In February the following year KDKA in Pittsburgh took its microphones to a theater and broadcast a play from there. The play was *Friend Mary*. So although WLW was first in a lot of things, it was not first in radio drama. WLW, though, was in there fast. A month after WGY broadcast its play, WLW presented what is termed "near drama." This means that Fred Smith, Robert Stayman, and the play's authoress Mary MacMillan got together in the WLW studio and read her play *A Fan and Two Candlesticks*. The next week, Mary Sullivan Brown read the balcony scene from *Romeo and Juliet*. Lots of plays were presented after that, even one by Fred Smith himself, *When Love Awakens*. Pretty soon everybody at WLW was talking about *radarios*.

[23]

What are *radarios?* Well, for one thing, they aren't any-more. Robert Stayman—announcer, actor, and editor of the *Crosley Radio Weekly*—made up the word to describe what Fred Smith was trying to do dramatically over WLW. The word probably comes from the word "radio" and the word "scenario" and WLW even tried to copyright it, but no matter. The word is now a part of history's trivia. One of Mr. Smith's original radarios was a musical called *When Madam Sings.* The plot was simple: a great opera star would not appear before a microphone because she couldn't find her powder puff and because her nose was shiny. Chil-dren's plays were presented, too. In 1923, *Writer's Digest* Editor T. C. O'Donnel heard one of his plays presented. It was *The Magic Journey.* Also, there were dramatic read-ings, usually by Fred Smith and usually classics that every-body and his brother loved. For background music, Ade-laide Apfel played the piano. All this and the Australian crawl!

WLW got so involved in putting on dramas that Mr. Crosley went all out and hired Helen Schuster Martin of the Schuster Martin Dramatic School to direct the plays that were broadcast. The school itself, one of the oldest of the kind in the United States, had been formed in 1900. Originally it was called a "School of Expression." Tyrone Power was one of its later graduates. So was Duane Snod-grass. So was Frank Bingham. By the time WLW hired Mrs. Martin, the station had fourteen actors who regularly appeared in its "radio stock company." Mrs. Thomie Prewitt Williams of the then Cincinnati Conservatory of Music was the musical director for the dramas. Later, William Stoess was.

News did not play too important role in those early days

of broadcasting, but now and then some news was broadcast. Radio stations back then had no reporters of their own. They had none of the wire services that are available today. Mostly, the announcers told about the weather and how the stock market was doing and what hogs were bringing in the Cincinnati market. Some news, though, could be covered, like election returns. During the November elections in 1922 a WLW staff member telephoned the returns from the Hamilton County election headquarters to the WLW studios where an announcer repeated them over the air. There were, also, occasional "news bulletins," like in that same November when a huge fire erupted at the Cincinnati waterfront, causing four riverboats to burn to the water's edge. Said the *Crosley Radio Weekly*:

"Up-to-the-minute details in regard to the spreading of the flames were broadcast before news of the fire became known through the publication of extra editions of newspapers, and long before associations were able to send dispatches to other cities."

According to Lawrence Wilson Lichty's research for his thesis, "Probably the biggest news flash was broadcast by WLW in August of 1923. Between musical numbers played by a band, Fred Smith went to the microphone and said, 'We are making an announcement that is the saddest ever given from WLW. President Harding died at 10:30 tonight.' That night Mr. Smith signed the station off around midnight, by saying: 'This day, August 2, 1923, will be a memorable one, because President Harding has just died. Do we not express the sentiment of the nation when we say—God's will be done? Good night.'"

There was another time that Fred Smith was upset. That was when WLW was first on the air in 1922. The station would pause now and then so that listeners could telephone in requests for recorded music. After playing a fistful of opera selections that he loved, Fred Smith was most upset when every request telephoned in, except one, was for jazz. He gritted his teeth and played jazz.

Had you listened in those days, you would have heard few commercials because, simply put, there weren't any. Technically from 1922 to 1926, WLW did not sell "commercial time" at all. There was no word from the sponsor because there was no sponsor. The man who owned the station sponsored the whole shooting match. Powel Crosley, Jr., wanted his radio station to succeed because it would help him sell radio sets. Simple as that. Of course, there were "mentions." Westheimer and Company got credit for supplying the stock market information. Baldwin got mentioned for supplying the piano. Drama schools got mentioned for supplying the dramatic talent. Had Izzy Kadetz—and not his pappy—been operating in those days, Izzy would have got credit for supplying the kosher corned beef sandwiches. And, of course, every time you turned around, you heard the name *Crosley* mentioned. There was the *Crosley* orchestra playing your favorite tune. There was the *Crosley* this and the *Crosley* that. So when you went to buy yourself a new radio, you had a pretty good idea of the name *Crosley*. That's why Crosley wanted to keep boosting power, as suggested earlier. The better the station, the better the reception—and the more radio receiving sets he sold.

If you think WLW's 50,000 watts today are powerful stuff, you probably will not be terribly impressed—as Cincinnati was back in 1923—when WLW boosted its power to 500 watts. But back then 500 watts was really something, if you will forgive us for being technical. By 1923 WLW was broadcasting remotes from the now departed Sinton Hotel. It also broadcast opera "live" from the Cincinnati Zoo. For those of you unfamiliar with Cincinnati, note that opera at the zoo is an accepted thing around here. But all was not perfect in those early days. On March 11, 1923, along came a big wind and poof! there went the antenna and the station was off the air for several days. In January, 1923, Crosley had purchased the Precision Instrument Company, Cincinnati, and as part of the purchase, acquired WMH which had, after a fashion, been on the air since 1919. The original WMH equipment can best be described as Mickey Mouse. The powerful little 10-watter's antenna was a vertical steel rod which had for an insulator at its base an empty wine bottle! By acquiring the station and the wine bottle, Crosley was able to have WLW itself on the air five nights a week instead of the three it had been allowed.

Just as your PTA group has a "theme" these days every time it tries to palm baked goods off on the public, so did radio in those early days have "themes." They were called "special nights." Fred Smith gets the credit for thinking them up. One night would be the "Radio Party Night" which meant you invited your friends and neighbors in to "ooh" and "ah" over the wonders of wireless. Or there would be "Hoosier Night" which meant, I suppose, that only those in Indiana or from Indiana were permitted to listen. Also, because the Hotel Sinton let WLW bring its microphones there to do remotes, there would be a "Hotel Sinton Night" and the talent, of course, would be arranged for by the hotel. And, when hard-pressed to come up with a winner, Fred Smith scheduled a "Miscellaneous

Night" which meant just what you think it means so break out a new batch of piano rolls and start pumping.

Later one of the nights was *really* special. WLW broadcast the wedding of Alice Hazenfield and William F. Mains. There was a beauty contest mixed up with the ceremonies somehow, with the beauty contest winners getting to be the honorary bride's maids. Other radio stations had "radio weddings," too.

In 1924 WLW made plans to increase its power again. This time it wanted to broadcast with 1,000 *watts!* The plan called for moving its transmitter and tower to Harrison, Ohio. Harrison is a pleasant community that straddles the Ohio-Indiana border, thus sharing the best—or worst—of two worlds. WLW, by then, could be found at 710 on your dial (now it is at 700). It shared the 710 dial position with WMH—not the one we met earlier that had the wine bottle, but another and newer one, the forerunner of today's WKRC. Confusion prevailed at times as the result of this sharing the dial position. Neither station could agree on which one should broadcast when. The result was, for several weeks, on Monday and Wednesday nights they both broadcast at the same time at the same place on the dial. Listeners, properly bewildered, screamed to Washington for help.

Says Lichty in his survey of the situation, "Secretary of Commerce Herbert Hoover ordered D. B. Carson, Commissioner of Navigation, and W. D. Terrell, chief radio supervisor, to go to Cincinnati on February 13, 1925. *The New York Times* editorialized the next day: 'It is hoped that the Secretary has the power as well as the wisdom to settle the controversy justly as well as promptly.' The newspaper further suggested that the best way the problem might be resolved was to 'toss a copper.' . . . WLW conceded an early period on Wednesday evening to WMH. But from 8 P.M. to 10 P.M. on Wednesday it was arranged that WMH would divide time with WLW for one month on 422.3 meters (710 kc) and the following month it would divide time with WSAI on 329.5 meters (920 kc). Thus, WMH on alternate months broadcast Wednesday night *on a different frequency.*"

The words are Lichty's but the italics are mine. That shows the way radio was back there in the less complicated (less complicated?) days. A year later found WLW broadcasting more than forty hours a week. But still you had to have the mind of a bookie to keep the hours straight. For example, WLW was "silent" on Friday nights. On Sundays, it signed off at 9:30 P.M. On Saturdays it signed off at 10 P.M. Also, on Monday and Thursday nights the station was off the air from nine to ten. Radio was there, but you had to look for it. And, as noted, now and then you got more than you bargained for—like two stations at once.

But as we approach the mid-twenties, we find the networks coming along to cheer us. As an example, say, of the 1926-27 season there was the *Eveready Hour, Atwater Kent Hour, Cities Service Concert, A&P Gypsies, Cliquot Club Eskimos, Jones & Hare, Reverend S. Parkes Cadman, Betty Crocker, Dr. Royal S. Copeland,* and as much or more rural music than you could possibly endure. The next season (1927-28) found us cranked into such favorites as *The True Story Hour, Great Moments in History, Cheerio,* and *The Dutch Masters Minstrels.* A season later (1929-30) we have *The Cuckoo Hour, The Nitwit Hour, Floyd Gibbons, Radio Guild Dramas, Amos 'n' Andy, Sherlock Holmes, The Adventures of Helen and Mary,* and that

[29]

all-time favorite of prepubescent smackheads, *The Lady Next Door*.

But when asked about the *kinds* of programs he wanted to give his listeners, Powel Crosley, Jr., back in 1926, said, "The programs broadcast during the winter will continue to feature dance orchestras and thematic programs of classical and semi-classical music. In addition to these, organ recitals, speeches of prominent men, old-time music, church services, special studio stunts and drama will be put on the air." By "thematic programs," he meant programs built around themes such as music of a certain country. Two years later, in 1928, he said, "We try to arrange our programs from morning to night on the basis of having the bulk of the material please the average taste, and a small remainder so diversified as to give a little bit of those things that please a smaller percentage of the audience."

On Wednesday, June 1, 1927, WLW moved from 710 to 700 on the dial. At first WLW shared this dial position with WMAF, Dartmouth, Massachusetts, and KFBU, Laramie, Wyoming. The Dartmouth station, though, operated only during the summer months and soon stopped operating at all. The Laramie station was eventually moved to another frequency. And now there WLW sits, 700 on your dial, a clear-channel station, the only one you'll ever find there, unless—that is—some Dartmouth wags sneak WMAF back on the air.

By 1927 WLW was not only getting programs from the network, but giving programs to the network as well. One program fed from the National Broadcasting Company's "Red" network was *The Crosley Hour*. The program, naturally, peddled Crosley radios to the workingman. Featured on the program was the Moscow Art Orchestra, just

[30]

the fare to capture the imagination of the laborer. Over WLW, listeners in this area heard Graham McNamee and Phillips Carlin describe the prize fight between Dempsey and Sharkey. But as the twenties dwindled to an end, there were some staff changes at WLW. For instance, Fred Smith bid WLW goodbye. The parting was an amiable one.

Fred Smith had almost single-handedly created the program schedule for WLW during its formative years. One of the programs was a news documentary broadcast. He had to create it. No news services were available to radio then. One of his earliest "news" programs had been an item called 'Musical News" which meant between musical selections he would toss in news items he had read in the newspapers and the magazines of the period. After each "news item" the organist would try to play a musical selection that seemed to tie in with the story. Said *Popular Radio* magazine, September, 1925, "WLW is using a novel method to present the daily news, and while it may not be very exciting as excitment is measured in these days of petting parties and uncovered feminine knees, it is pretty good for so young and yet so mossy a thing as radio broadcasting."

In 1928, Fred Smith carried his news idea further. Given the weekly chore of writing a "news roundup" for WLW, he chanced upon the news magazines, like *Time*, and rewrote from their material. He then submitted the idea of the broadcast to *Time* itself. September 3, 1928, *Time* began a service to radio stations, sending them ten-minute newscasts—for a price, of course. As many as 110 stations carried these *Time* "news roundups" and the program bore the title "newscasting." Several years later, in 1931, Fred

[31]

Smith himself moved on to the *Time* organization, being one of the first writers for *The March of Time* in which news events were dramatized weekly. So Fred Smith was gone. "*Time marches on.* . . ."

WLW was getting all kinds of programs from everywhere, many still local originations. It is said the first transcribed program carried by WLW was *Amos 'n' Andy*, originating from WMAQ, Chicago. Later, the program was carried live via the network.

And WLW was going everywhere, too. Around January, 1925, the station began tinkering with its new 5,000-watt transmitter at the Harrison, Ohio, site. WLW was the first station in the United States to use this much power. Said *Popular Radio* magazine, July, 1925, WLW "may be heard any time in the evening throughout the United States and in many foreign countries." By September, 1925, four other stations were also using 5,000 watts. A year after getting on the air with 5,000 watts, though, WLW ordered a 50,000-watt transmitter and here we go again!

"I am looking forward to the day," Mr. Crosley said in 1925, "when first class broadcasting stations will use from 50 to 100 kilowatts (50,000 to 100,000 watts). I believe this is as essential as it was for commercial companies figuratively to boost the power of the original one-half kilowatt used by Marconi when he sent the famous letter 'S' across the Atlantic Ocean to 50 kilowatts and later, 200 kilowatts, for satisfactory transoceanic communications. . . . The quality of service rendered by the high-powered stations should be recognized by the Department of Commerce in assignment of wave-lengths, and this recognition should necessarily have coupled with it, certain requirements as to quality of service. . . . There must be more recognition of quality of service and priority than there has been heretofore. First-class stations should not be asked to divide time with third-class ones. . . . Though still untried, I believe more strongly than ever in super-power. . ."

On May 25, 1928, WLW was authorized to start building its 50,000-watt transmitter. By then, Mr. Crosley had made arrangements to buy WSAI. WSAI's Mason, Ohio, transmitter site was available, and so that ended Harrison, Ohio, as a great radio center. On October 4, 1928, WLW cranked up its transmitter and there it was, talking at the world with a 50,000-watt shout that originated from Mason, Ohio. Among those on the October 29 dedication program were Cincinnati Mayor Murray Seasongood, Mr. Crosley himself, and a host of WLW staff members. These included the William Stoess Orchestra, Tom Richley, Louis John Johnen, Mabel Johnson, the Humming Trio, Weyland Echols, George Conver, Ida Blackson, the Frohne Sisters, the Burnt Corkers, Henry Theis' Hotel Sinton Orchestra, the Crosley Cossacks, Garber's Swiss Garden Orchestra, Pat Gillick, the Variety Three, the Office Boys, Leo Underhill, the Gondolyrics, Fred Roehr, Rhiney Gau, Harvey Brownfield (Bruce's dad), Don Dewey, Don Becker, plus Lucille and Mary. Plus others! The NBC network carried an hour of the celebration. Most of the celebration was broadcast from the Crosley studios, but at the Sinton Hotel there was (wheee) a "radio frolic."

The new power meant new transmitting facilities at Mason, Ohio. Short wave buffs please note that the station installed a pair of three hundred foot towers, six hundred feet apart, with the antenna stretched horizontally between the two on a north-south line. Whereas the 5,000 watt

[33]

transmitter had been water-cooled, the 50,000 transmitter was also water-cooled, but the water was in turn cooled by five giant fans. As for coverage, both Washington, D.C., and Jacksonville, Florida, said WLW came in as powerful as any local on the dial. WOR in New York complained a little. Said the New York station: WLW at 700 on the dial was causing a little interference with it at 710 on the dial. This was the moment in time that WLW became "The Nation's Station."

And, peeping at us just around the corner, is 1929 and the doings of Wall Street.

The Crosley Radio Corporation had a good thing going in 1928. The company made a net profit of nearly four million dollars. In 1929, however, the net profit was a little more than one million. The upcoming depression did not cause all of this decline. The market for radio receivers had leveled off. Those who wanted one, had one. Those who thought about getting one found, sometimes, they were out of work and could not afford one. Some could not even afford the "Pup" which was a one-tube set Crosley first shipped off to the marketplace in the waning months of 1925. And, in the excitement of playing with WLW, he had to set aside—temporarily—his first love: manufacturing automobiles. But that dream was just around the corner and so was a new refrigerator.

By the time the twenties ended, Powel Crosley, Jr., had established his mark on WLW and WLW had established its mark on Cincinnati and as far out there beyond as the airwaves carried its signal. But radio had matured. Gone were the quick and easy days of shouting into the morning glory horn microphone. Gone were the days when performers who strolled in from the street—or were waylaid as they passed near—were put before the microphones in that first hot and stuffy little studio that contained the transmitter as well. Gone were the days of the freight train engineer playing steam-whistle countermelody to those who would sing opera.

When the twenties ended, DX'ing had ended for all but the newest radio listener. The listener wanted programs. The listener no longer was a member of the "Lightning Bugs." The lightning bugs had winked off. And what was left, was radio.

CUE the thirties.

Cue the Great Depression, the 1937 flood in the Ohio Valley, Roosevelt's Fireside Chats, the first streamlined passenger train, the repeal of Prohibition, Will Rogers ("We are the first nation in the history of the world to go to the poor house in an automobile!"), the Blue Eagle, Kate Smith coming over the mountain ("Hello, everybody!"), Fibber McGee's closet, Ma Perkins, people selling apples on street corners, the dust bowl, the Okies heading west to the Promised Land, Little Orphan Annie ("Leapin' Lizards!"), Tom Mix, Tarzan, Buck Rogers, Shirley Temple, John Dillinger, Machine Gun Kelly, the *real* Bonnie and Clyde (they were Mr. and Mrs. Clyde Barrow), Eleanor Roosevelt (and Anna and James and Elliott and Franklin, Jr., and John), the CCC, the PWA, the WPA, Brenda Frazier, Aly Khan, John L. Lewis ("Labor, like Israel, has many sorrows!"), the union sit-ins, Jane Withers, Clark Gable, Jean Harlow, Fred Astaire and

Ginger Rogers, the Marx Brothers, *Snow White and the Seven Dwarfs, Gone With the Wind,* Father Charles E. Coughlin, "Moon Over Miami," and—while you're at it—cue the organist to give us a little of "Caprice Viennoise," then hold under, and cue Peter Grant, who will say:

> *Down the valley of a thousand yesterdays*
> *Flow the bright waters of Moon River,*
> *On and on, forever waiting to carry you*
> *Down to the land of forgetfulness,*
> *To the kingdom of sleep.*
> *To the realm of*
> *Moon River,*
> *A lazy stream of dreams*
> *Where vain desires forget themselves*
> *In the loveliness of sleep.*
> *Moon River,*
> *Enchanting white ribbon*
> *'Twined in the hair of night*
> *Where nothing is but sleep.*
> *Dream on, sleep on*
> *Care will not seek for thee,*
> *Float on, drift on,*
> *Moon River . . . to the sea.*

Wow! The *wow* is mine, but the mood—and the memory —belongs strictly to WLW. Although Peter Grant went down to the sea a lot with *Moon River,* he was not the only announcer to recite its poetry. Harry Holcomb did. And so did Palmer Ward, Charles Woods, Don Dowd, Jay Jostyn, Jimmy Leonard, and Ken Linn. They say that once Ken Linn "broke" the sweet and romantic format by reciting *The Shooting of Dan McGrew* at the lovers out there in radioland. John Clark fired him fast, but hired him back again just as fast when, according to the story, the poem had been requested via cable from the Duchess of Edinburgh. *Moon River*, at the time, was heard everywhere because that was in the thirties and WLW broadcast with 500,000 watts.

If anything, *Moon River* typifies the WLW of the thirties. The story of its origin shows how radio was back then. The *Moon River* program began in 1930. Its creator was Edward Byron. Or was its creator Powel Crosley, Junior? Each had a hand in it, so did a WLW violinist. Mary Wood, columnist for the *Cincinnati Post & Times-Star* who served her time as a WLW writer and got off with good behavior, tells of the start of *Moon River*.

"Eddie Byron told me himself," she recalls. "It seems that up on Court Street during those Prohibition Days there was this place you could get a beer or whatever might interest you from the waitresses because it is rumored the place was run by a madam. Every night, after WLW signed off, Eddie and some of the staff musicians would go there for beer. Well, one day Crosley called Eddie into his office and told Eddie he had just purchased a new organ for WLW. It was the organ he dedicated to his mother. Also he told Eddie, 'Beginning tomorrow night I'd like to have a nice program at midnight, featuring organ music and poety. Nice *soft* music and poetry. You'll need a nice theme song and a poem to get the program going. Oh, and have it on the air tomorrow night.' That was the way Crosley was: he wanted things done yesterday. After Eddie closed up the station that night he went down to join his friends for a beer. The WLW staff violinist was with him, playing music to entertain the beer drinkers and the ladies in attendance. While the rest of them relaxed and enjoyed themselves, Eddie drank beer and scribbled dozens of false starts on paper. After much beer, according to Eddie, what he wrote began to sound pretty good to him. So he recited it to the ladies while the violinist played "Caprice Viennoise" in the background. There the ladies were, all in their kimonos, weeping. That was when Eddie knew he had a winner. And *that* was where *Moon River* was conceived."

Bob Brown was the first to send the listeners down to the sea, but because he wasn't at his best with poetry, he was quickly replaced—in less than a week of getting in the hair of night—by Harry Holcomb. Eddie Byron, having originated *Famous Jury Trials* while in the writing bullpen at WLW, moved onto New York where he created *Mr. District Attorney*. Other writers on WLW's *Famous Jury Trials* were Milton Kramer, Len Finger, Daisy Amoury, Lawrence Menkin, Bill Rafael, Martin Young, Stedman Coles, Paul Monash, Ameel Fisher, Jerry McGill, and Joseph Greene. The announcers were Peter Grant and Hugh James. Jean Paul King was one of the actors. So was True Boardman.

The thirties were heady—and cramped—days for the WLW writers. As writers are when collected together for a common purpose (to write an ad for mouthwash, to write a speech for the President, or to write another chapter for *Ma Perkins*) they are unattended free spirits that had better not be left unattended for too long. Many writers have passed through the WLW stables. Some have passed through more quickly than others. The afore-mentioned Mary Wood was in that collection of writers for the thirties. She says she was first there in 1934. She has given up trying to recall *all* the program directors that WLW had in those days. "At one time," she said, "a program director lasted two months which made us proud of him because he had set some kind of record. We had a staff of writers then that sounded like the Notre Dame starting lineup. One of them, who later wrote for *Ma Perkins*, was our leading communist. He was like our guru. Every Saturday night all the writers would gather in an apartment, drink gin, and talk each other into enlisting in the Abraham Lincoln Brigade fighting in Spain. But none of us did. Monday morning would find all of us back in the WLW bullpen, writing drama that would tear your heart out. Our motto was: 'Nothing is so bad today that it can't get worse tomorrow.'"

One writer, who later went on to produce *Captain Video* on television, had the chore of writing a fifteen minute monster serial for the WLW children listeners. He would show up at the Arlington Street studios in the morning, write that afternoon's episode, and then wander off somewhere to drink and talk of poetry. Unfortunately, one Thursday he got so enthused with poetry—or drink—that he failed to appear at the studio on Friday morning to create that day's episode. When the Thursday episode had ended, a demented woods monster—a woodsman who had gone back to nature, snarled a lot, and didn't think too straight—had been pounding on the cabin door behind which huddled the lovely young heroine. When the cast gathered for Friday's episode, there were no scripts and there was no time to write one. So they all muddled through as best they could. The Friday episode consisted of the girl, trapped in the cabin, screaming during the whole broadcast, plus the snarls of the demented woods monster, plus the soundman, making door-pounding noises.

Did the writer get fired? It is not known. But what is known is that at WLW people got fired a lot. Singer Barbara Cameron claims to hold the record. She was fired four different times. But talent in those days was always available. It was the moment of stock companies—traveling actors and actresses—and it was the moment of the tight dollar. Road shows used to get stranded in Cincinnati, the actors would hire out at WLW to get enough cash to get back home, and some of them, liking the idea of radio, stayed around.

You can't blame Powel Crosley, Jr., for the revolving door policy at WLW. Few of the employees did. To them, for the most part, he was the tall and balding fellow who seemed more interested in the mechanical aspects of radio—and building cars—than he was in the broadcast side of the business. He left programming to those whom he felt knew programming—and if they didn't prove themselves, he fired them. Life was that simple. He had such an abiding faith—and perhaps awe—of creative artists that he was wise enough to let them alone. But he was forever discovering talent. Jane Froman was one of his discoveries. She had been studying at the Conservatory of Music. Since she was a friend of his daughter, he had heard her sing in his home. He got her on the air. And the rest is history, like for instance, the demented woods creature pounding on the cabin door.

To be a businessman, as Crosley was, and to be surrounded by hypersensitive artists, some with and some without talent, did pose a problem now and then. There was the bewildering moment for Mr. Crosley when he brought several male and female dinner guests to visit his pride and joy, the WLW studios on Arlington Street. Trouble is, for weeks prior, both announcers and engineers had been trying their best to "break" Peter Grant on the air and to make him laugh. Couldn't be done, but they kept trying, getting more far-fetched each try. Each night, when Peter Grant read the ten o'clock news over WLW, the others stood before him, doing a striptease complete with bumps and grinds. No reaction from Peter Grant. He just kept on reading. One night they went all out. They did a strip for real. And there they were, down to their socks, grinding away; and there Peter Grant was, unperturbed, reading the news; and *there* through the studio door came Crosley and his entourage of dinner guests . . .

It is easy to see why Mr. Crosley, chose to leave the creative matters to creative people, isn't it?

Barbara Cameron, the wonderful singer who holds the record of being fired the most from WLW, also holds another kind of record: collecting cash for staying home and listening to herself on radio. This began in the days of *Moon River* when the DeVore Sisters were the vocalists. Actually, most girl singers at WLW took turns getting into the hair of night and sloshing to the sea. Doris Day used to sing on *Moon River*. So did the Clooney sisters, Betty and Rosemary. So did Janette Davis, Lucille Norman, Anita Ellis, Ruby Wright, Bonnie Lou and—to get a male voice in there—Phil Brito. Point is, when one of the DeVore sisters got married and left the hair of night to others, Barbara Cameron was elected to fill out the musical group. This was a moment in time when *Moon River* was recorded and peddled to other cities, one of them being a southern city, its sponsor there a mattress manufacturer. Later, after Barbara Cameron had left WLW one of her several times, she was sitting at home, cranked into the station, and heard *herself* still on *Moon River*. She listened patiently to herself perform for nearly a year, realizing the station was rerunning some of the old transcriptions of former *Moon River* programs. Finally, she sent WLW a bill for her services. Poor WLW had to pay, because— simply put—that is the way the union things are: performers are to be paid for their efforts whenever the station uses those efforts, whether "live" or from the library of yesteryear.

Crosley had problems with another performer, Fats Waller. According to *Cincinnati Magazine*, March 1968, "(Crosley's) temper once cost him the greatest of all WLW stars, Fats Waller. Waller, who had a predilection for black derbies, cigars, and gin, also happened to be one of the greatest jazz pianists of all times. He particularly coveted an organ in the main studio of the radio station which Crosley had dedicated to his late mother. One night Crosley walked into the station and found Waller, in derby and cigar, playing one of his own compositions, 'Ain't Misbehavin',' on the organ. Enraged, Crosley accused Waller of desecrating his mother's memory and fired him on the spot. Waller went on to greater things, but the organ never played right until one day a cleaning lady moved it out to dust and was deluged by empty gin bottles which rolled out across the floor."

Ah, but those were great days. In the thirties WLW used, as we suggest, 500,000 watts of power, got *Moon River* requests from Europe, and—as Mary Wood recalls —WLW blanketed the world. Around here, you didn't

[44]

even need a radio to hear it. Turn on a faucet and out came WLW!"

Heady days! On May 2, 1934, President Franklin Delano Roosevelt pushed a gold key on his White House desk (the same key President Wilson had used to open the Panama Canal twenty years before) and *that* was the moment, exactly at 9:30 P.M., the 500,000 watts of WLW were to activate themselves. Didn't quite work out that way, though. As the President was saying:

"I have just pressed the key to formally open Station WLW. It has been a pleasure to do this . . ."

Well, the 500,000 watt transmitter tubes were still warming up. But no matter, it is the thought that counts. WLW was then the most powerful radio station in the world, coming out of radios and water faucets everywhere.

Said Powel Crosley, Jr., that evening that meant so much to him, "It has been our ambition to increase WLW's power from time to time as rapidly as technical obstacles could be overcome in order to bring the voice of this station to those in remote parts of the country who might experience difficulty in getting good reception because of interference of static and other atmospheric disturbances. With each increase in power a large number of people have come to rely on WLW for the things that only radio can bring into their homes. With this greater and greater audience has come greater and greater responsibilities. The programs of this station must be built to please the greatest number of people possible. It must be regarded as a public service and always operate as such. We feel fully this responsibility to our listeners and I pledge again that we shall continue the operation of WLW for the good of the listening public."

If you are the sort that goes around putting a penny in the fuse box, you will not be terribly interested in the technical side of cranking up a transmitter so it sends out 500,-000 watts. But bear with us. We weren't either until we looked into the matter. For instance, the new transmitter used *twenty* 100,000-watt tubes, not the sort you'd find in the tube-rack at your local drug store. These tubes got hot so they were cooled by water, five hundred gallons of water each minute to be exact. This was distilled water as in your electric steam iron. This water in turn got hot and had to be cooled by seven hundred gallons of tap water each minute. So the city itself would not run out of water, WLW built a pond seventy-five feet square near the transmitter to re-cool the tap water and use it over and over again. The pond, as noted elsewhere, never froze over in the winter and small wonder! Radio hams will be pleased to note that six mercury vapor rectifier tubes rated at 450 amperes were used in the transmitter, the modulation transformers weighed in at near fifty tons and contained fourteen hundred gallons of oil. The 500,000-watt transmitter used each year nearly 15,500,000 kilowatt hours of electricity, enough—they say—to light a hundred thousand-person city based on 1934 rates of consumption. The antenna was new, too. Most broadcast stations started out with horizontal antennae, a line swaying in the air between two towers. By the time WLW came on the air with 500,000 watts, only four or five other radios were using vertical antennae: a tower, that is, straight up in the sky, from which the broadcast signal was radiated. The new antenna at WLW stood 831 feet tall, cost $46,243 to build, and changed forever the flight of sparrows. More than two hundred tons of downward pressure from the

[46]

guy wires support it from the pushing and shoving of the wind. On a hot day, the tower "grows." It grows as much as six inches. The tower itself weighed 136 tons. All of this tower weight rested on a piece of porcelain shaped like a cup.

But the new power posed nasty engineering problems, as has been suggested. So much power radiated from the tower that in some homes in nearby Mason the house lights would *not* turn off. It was also learned, though it was no surprise to the non-technical gaping at the thing, that the high tower was a dandy lightning rod. A special relay—or cut-off—was rigged. Operated by an electric eye, it managed to turn off the transmitter's plate voltage to the final amplifier—whenever lightning decided to have an electric go at the tower. So much for beginning electricity.

For those who attended the dedicatory program that caused the Mason householders to have nonstop electric lighting, note that the toastmaster for the evening was Charles Sawyer, then Lieutenant Governor of Ohio. Shrimp cocktail Louisiana was served, so was music by the Crosley Symphony under the direction of William Stoess. Grace Clauve Raine directed the Crosley Glee Club, guests ate filet of beef, and along came Henry Thies and his Purol (sic) Orchestra *and* Virginio Marucci and his South Americans, he being the fiddle player who, along with Ed Byron, created the *Moon River* mood that long-ago night, causing the maidens in attendance to weep.

The sheer *power* of WLW then created problems, other than in Mason, Ohio. By the autumn of 1934, CFRB in Toronto, Canada, but right next door to WLW on the dial (WLW at 700, CFRB at 690) complained that WLW was causing interference, mostly at night. So four days before Christmas of that year, the Federal Communication Commission ruled that WLW could still broadcast 500,000 during the daylight hours, every direction, but at night it would have to be more directional, or stop playing. WLW went directional at night. In doing so, its engineering staff created another broadcasting first: the first *directional* antenna ever created for vertical angle suppression. Thus, the antenna as modified, protected the Canadian station from nighttime interference while at the same time did not change dramatically its basic groundwave service. Engineers will be glad to explain this to you. Other stations complained a little, too. WOR in New York was one of them. WOR *then* being in Newark, New Jersey. And down in Louisiana there was a broadcaster named Henderson who used to complain on the air about WLW's new power and, some suggest, that now and then he used strong language on the air to register his complaints, but we have no record of this.

Even before WLW became a super power in the thirties, it branched out into another area: that of *commercial* broadcasting. The first year WLW itself ever made a profit was in 1930. In the period ending March 31, 1931 WLW had made a net profit of $43,464. A year later, it made a net profit of $145,868. *Merchandising* was one of the reasons for WLW's early success and present success in broadcasting, at least insofar as its continuing amiable relationship with advertisers goes. According to *Broadcasting* Magazine, May 15, 1932, "The first successful merchandising service for clients of a broadcasting station is claimed by J. L. Clark, general manager of WLW, Cincinnati. The service is provided through J. Ralph Corbett, Inc., Cincinnati, which has field men in Indianapolis,

Columbus, and Wheeling. The service is provided both national and local sponsors within the primary zone of WLW. It includes the contacting of jobbers and dealers and merchandising the radio programs. Dealers are encouraged to identify themselves with the broadcasts."

John Clark had been moved by Mr. Crosley over from other portions of the Crosley business to the radio end. He came in when radio—and especially WLW—had room for innovators. He innovated a lot. He fired some people, too. No matter. So did everybody else.

Meanwhile, back in front of the microphones, drama was. It was actually in 1930 that Edward Armour Byron, whom we have met several times earlier in this chapter, operating as WLW production manager, helped create a stock company of actors at WLW. He was practical, too. Why, he thought, waste time and money by doing a drama on the radio only once? So, when the *Crosley Theater of the Air* started in the fall of 1930, the plays were broadcast first late Thursday evening, repeated early Saturday evening, and then one more time on Sunday afternoons. In the first two years the *Crosley Theater of the Air* was in existence, it broadcast eighty original dramas, light and heavy and those reworked somehow from the classics. Also the same crew cranked out two rural dramas a week, entitled *Centerville Sketches*. And for one wonderful season, late at night, those who tuned in heard wonderful Sidney Ten Eyck and his *Doodlesockers* program. He wrote it himself. He was the forerunner of Bob and Ray, Henry Morgan, Ransom Sherman, and just about every good radio humorist who ever lighted the airwaves. He was good. He didn't last too long, though.

It was also in the thirties that WLW went up into the

[49]

skies—almost. Crosley, who had a secret love for airplanes as well as automobiles, bought a Lockheed-Vega racing plane, equipped it with broadcast gear that was a 150-watt radio station and announcer Robert Brown, and sent the whole shooting match up in the sky with a pilot to fly around Cincinnati, look down, and say how pretty things were below. Mr. Crosley also entered the plane called *New Cincinnati* in the National Air Races but the plane, having the added weight of the broadcast equipment plus announcer Robert Brown, came in fourth. In case you're keeping score, Wiley Post won. Broadcasts from the plane were picked up by stations along the race path from the West Coast to Chicago. But the radio transmitter went out, the announcer burned himself trying to fix it, and to make a long story short, it wasn't a roaring success. Mr. Brown returned to earth and stayed, a much happier man.

And there was that charming little old lady who owned the lumberyard in Rushville Center standing around waiting in the wings. Her name? Well, her real name was Virginia Payne. Her other name—and just as real—was *Ma Perkins.*

In 1934 you could have heard an hour and a half of soap operas on WLW. In 1937, three years later, you could have heard four and a half hours of soap operas on WLW. This is each and every day, Monday through Friday, of course. During the period of World War II, WLW carried seven hours of soap operas a day. As time went on, of course, most of the "soaps" were originated by the networks from Chicago and New York. But in the thirties, WLW originated some of its own, as well, perhaps, as originating the art-form itself. The would-be revolutionists in the WLW writing bull pen turned out daily episodes for the WLW serials: *Ma Perkins, The Life of Mary Sothern,* and *The Mad Hatterfields. Ma Perkins* had a staying power. She stuck around until November 25, 1960, when after twenty-seven years and 7,065 broadcasts of slow-motion but compelling life in Rushville Center, she wasn't any more. *The Life of Mary Sothern* was written mostly by Don Becker and it featured Minabelle Abbott. A WLW origination, it was the first "soap" ever to be carried on the Mutual network. *The Mad Hatterfields* was cranked out by Pauline Hopkins. Among those taking the roles were Allen Franklyn, Betty Lee Arnold, Bess McCammon, Harry Cansdale, and William Green.

There are those spoilsports who say that *Ma Perkins* was not the first soap opera and in reality, the spoilsports are right. The first five-day-a-week drama aimed at the housewife was probably NBC's *Clara, Lu and Em,* but one researcher goes back further to note that in 1928, in August to be exact, *Real Folks,* ran on the NBC-Blue network.

Ah, but say those who would give WLW more firsts than it could reasonably claim credit for, if not first with soaps, WLW was at least first with the dramatic program of the crime-detective type. They point with reasonable pride to *Dr. Konrad's Unsolved Mysteries* WLW writers and players created in 1933. But, others suggest, the first radio thriller of this sort was *Sherlock Holmes* which went on the air in or before 1931. And, others say, what about *The Shadow* which was broadcast in 1929? Only Lamont Cranston knows and he ain't talking. But it is interesting to note that Orson Wells once played the role of the *Shadow* on radio. And note that Agnes Moorehead once played the role of Margot Lane. Kenny Delmar was once Commissioner

Weston. And Keenan Wynn played Shrevie. So did Everett Sloan, Alan Reed, Mandel Kramer, and Bob Maxwell.

Anyway, by 1932, WLW had collected quite a bunch of people to entertain over the airwaves. In 1932 WLW had nearly a hundred musicians on the pay roll, half of them full-time. Every out-of-work or stranded actor or actress usually wandered into the Arlington Street studios, looking for a job. And out in the boondocks, at work on 250-watt coffeepots as little backwoods broadcast stations are some-times called, a thousand announcers looked upon WLW as Mecca—and WLW was. To work as a staff announcer at WLW these days has value, to be sure, but to be hired as a staff announcer at WLW radio in those days was the same as having your tonsils beatified. To those who said they had worked at WLW, every door of opportunity was open. To be an announcer at WLW was to be equal to or better than any network announcer ever to open his yap. They call this place the birthplace of the stars. The gang at WLW—now Avco—will recite you lists of names of the greats who had once appeared before the WLW microphones. Most of this list is correct. But even the WLW people, wonderful as they are, get carried away at times. *Did* Amos and Andy ever work here? Is *this* where they got their start? Our hearts say yes but our minds say no. They were *heard* over WLW, but they originated, some suggest, from WMAQ in Chicago. Is this where Red Skelton got his start in radio? Some say yes, some say no, and they are both right.

In the late thirties the wonderful Mr. Skelton used to travel to Cincinnati once a week to the WLW studios out on Arlington Street where he would rehearse and put on, for the network, a show called *Avalon Time*, named after a cigarette. I know because I used to steal out to the studios, press my nose against the glass, and watch with awe as he—soundlessly—went through the rehearsal. The glass was too thick for me to hear. Peter Grant was his announcer. Peter Grant had, in the thirties, come to WLW from St. Louis. Recalls Mr. Skelton, "Peter Grant sounded exactly like Franklin Roosevelt. We were told we had to take him off the air and I said, 'You can't take a man's livelihood away from him just because he sounds like the President.' Anyway, he changed his delivery and he stayed on with us."

I remember, I remember. . .

So Red Skelton did—and *didn't*—start here. He was never in the hire of WLW. He only came here to use its facilities to originate his show for the network. On the other hand, "Singing Sam" did originate at WLW. First he was "Singing Sam the Lawn-Mower Man." He went onto New York, they took his lawn-mower away, and he became "Singing Sam, the Barbasol Man." The Mills Brothers started here. So did Little Jack Little. So did a group who called themselves "The King, The Jack, and The Jester." You probably know them better as the "Inkspots." Red Barber started here as sportscaster, didn't he? And wasn't Durwood Kirby his announcer here? Some suggest that Crosley and WLW did the first quiz show, *Doctor I.Q.*, but the less said about that the better. "Smiling Ed McConnell" started here. And to more modern times, so did Rod Serling and—well, we were going to say Walt Phillips, but Walt got fired a lot. He might have started somewhere else. All that can be said is that he can be considered Mr. Radio in Chicago. Bill Nimmo started here, went on to New York, and came back again to marry Marian Spelman

who also got started on WLW—and don't they make a
wonderful couple? The McGuire Sisters might have started
here. Add Eddie Albert. Add Dick Noel. And in the next
chapter, we'll get Andy Williams into the act. Also, there's
Frank Lovejoy. He got started here, they say, as a stranded
actor who sought WLW comfort in the form of work.

Peter Grant didn't *start* here, but he lasted so long and
so well it seems as if he had always been here, doesn't it?

Also in the thirties—and even in the twenties—another
group came to WLW and made their mark. I'm speaking
of those who bring rosin, guitar picks, good cheer, rube
jokes, and country music. I'm speaking of the gang from
the present *Midwestern Hayride*—and from *all* the shows
WLW sent out over the wind to the folks back home. They
call themselves country music people now. Call them what
you will, country music people, hillbillies, or you name it.
Just call me when they start to play.

And. . .a. . .one. . .and. . .a. . .two. . .

I dreamed I was there,
In Hillbilly Heaven
Oh, what a beautiful sight.
I met all the stars,
In Hillbilly Heaven
*Oh, what a star-studded night.**

To those of you who have never heard Ernie Lee tell his wife to put on the coffee pot because he was coming home or who think Minnie Pearl is a fried chicken, or who are not sure whether Skeeter Davis is a girl or a guy, this chapter will mean little. If you know who Margie Bowes is, or if you have ever listened to Pa and Ma McCormick, hang in.

* *HillyBilly Heaven*, by Eddie Dean and Hal Southern; reprinted by permission of Sage and Sand Music, Inc., Copyright © 1954. All rights reserved.

There are those who say that hillbilly—or *country* music, if you prefer—means little. To them the Cincinnati Symphony Orchestra is where reality lies. But may we suggest that one has only to see Bonnie Lou bring out her banjo, kick off her shoes, and sing about the cotton fields back home to understand that many of us are country music people at heart? Bonnie Lou has lighted entire grandstands with her banjo-picking and her enthusiastic singing. And so have Pa and Ma McCormick since the early thirties on WLW. All you have to do around this area to conjure up more pleasant memories than you can shake a stick at is to recite some of those names of WLW talent past and present.

There's Buddy Ross, Shug Fisher, George Biggar, Merle Travis, Hal O'Halloran, Curly Fox and Texas Ruby, Lulubelle and Scotty, Millie and Dolly Good, Captain Stubby and the Buccaneers, Lazy Jim Day, and Roy Starkey. And, since we might as well mix television into this chapter of WLW and country music, do you remember wonderful Willie Thall as the master of ceremonies of the *Midwestern Hayride?* And do you remember when—of all people—Paul Dixon was the master of ceremonies? WLW radio and television have come a long long way since the early days of the *Boone County Jamboree* but oh, those days—all of them—remember so well!

"Hello," Boss Johnson used to say, "and how's everybody down on the farm?"

When he came on everybody down on the farm was just fine, thank you.

Time was when WLW used to "travel" its country music stars just about everywhere buses and trains could reach. A county fair in Ohio wasn't really a county fair unless someone from the country music staff was there, picking and a-singing.

According to Bill Sachs of *Billboard*, "Possibly the most concentrated string of fair bookings ever held down by a single attraction was that of WLW *Boone County Jamboree*, starting in the early forties and running for many years. Bill McCluskey, formerly with the WLS *National Barn Dance*, Chicago, left there at that time to handle the talent office for WLW. Under McCluskey's direction, the 'Boone County Jamboree' played some seventy-two fairs in the area covering Ohio, West Virginia, Pennsylvania, Indiana, and Kentucky. Forty-two of the fairs were in Ohio alone. . ."

Back in the early thirties, most of the hillbilly variety programs were heard in the morning on WLW, many before dawn, while outside the world was still dark with the dark of night. WLW was booming out guitar-pickings with its powerful 500,000 watt voice to just about every farm that had a radio and—in the vicinity of Mason, Ohio, where the 500,000-watt transmitter was—to some that didn't. Pa and Ma McCormick were no newcomers to the WLW microphone. They had been around the station since the late twenties. Some of their co-workers included Clyde J. Foley, better known as "Red," Roland Gaines, Millie and Dolly Good, and Bradley Kincaid. For down-on-the-farm rube comedy there was any announcer holding down the morning staff assignment. Others who appeared on WLW radio back then were Whitey "The Duke of Paducah" Ford, Lloyd "Cowboy" Copas, "Lazy" Jim Day, Bob Albright, Rex Griffith, the Drifting Pioneers, and Hugh Cross and his Radio Pals.

Do you remember what the morning program was called?

If you said *Top o' the Morning* you can go to the head of your class. Also in the thirties, right about the time of the awful 1937 flood which was the greatest thus far to trouble the Ohio Valley, the *Renfro Valley Barn Dance* started. This was broadcast over WLW. At first it was broadcast from the acoustically-perfect and cavernous Cincinnati Music Hall, but in November 1939, the whole shooting match was moved, rosin and all, to Rock Castle County, Kentucky. where it officially set up shop in Renfro Valley. John Lair, Red Foley, and Whitey Ford ran the programs which, later, were originated for the Columbia Broadcasting System network via WHAS, Louisville.

Also, as part of the 500,000 watts of something for everybody, WLW got involved with farm programs on a big scale. George Biggar, who came to WLW from Chicago's Prairie Farmer Station WLS and later went back to WLS, originated such programs as *Everybody's Farm Hour* and *Everybody's Farm News.* In 1941, Mr. Biggar actually developed the program *Everybody's Farm* from the farm in Mason, Ohio, where the WLW tower is. Programs were originated from "the little white studio" out there in the rural boondocks. The farm grew. It started out as 137 acres. Soon it boasted of 750 acres. Roy Battles became the farm director in 1944. Time was, the networks carried farm programs, for instance, NBC's *Farm and Home Hour.* The program began in 1928, but by the sixties, it had vanished.

WLW can't claim to be the inventor of country music programs on the airwaves. In 1925, George D. Hay—"The Solemn Old Judge"—started the *WLS Barn Dance* and the *WSM Barn Dance.* In 1927 the *National Barn Dance,* outgrowth of the *WLS Barn Dance,* used to follow Walter Damrosch and the National Symphony Orchestra on the network. They say that one evening the judge opened the *WSM Barn Dance* by saying, "For the past hour we have been listening to music taken largely from grand opera, but from now on we will present 'The Grand Ole Opry!' " The name stuck!

In the thirties, WLW cranked out a lot of country music —more than a dozen hours each week during the 1937-38 season. This was ten percent of WLW's programming. Some of the programs were, besides *Top o' the Morning, Brown County Revelers, Rural Roundup, Boone County Caravan, The Happy Valley Girls, The Plantation Boys, Lucky Penny Club, Trail Blazers,* and the *Prairie Ramblers.* These were local originations. In addition, the network pumped in *Carson Robinson's Buckeroo's, Reveille Round-up,* and *Chuck Acree.* Those were the good old days of the thirties and forties. By the mid-fifties, not a single radio show was left that had need of a guitar pick. Bob Shreve now sells us beer on the late night movie. The days of *Bob Shreve and the Swanee River Boys* are no more. In 1960, the *National Barn Dance* said goodbye. The theater was shuttered and dark and silent, filled with only ghost-whispers of rube jokes of yesteryear.

But the *Midwestern Hayride*—on the tube—is still with us. Does that help? And western music, with Japanese sub-titles, is boffo in the Orient. Also, many country music peo-ple have crossed over to rock. Billy Haley and the Comets, for instance, are really country music men turned modern. And so is Elvis Presley. And the Everley Brothers. But, oh the good old days! Sit a moment with Bill McCluskey and remember along with him. Bill McCluskey, of course, is that delightful bespectacled businessman who on St. Patrick's Day dances the Irish Jig on whatever WLW program that will have him—and they *all* will because he's rather special and rather wonderful. At present he has the title of Client Service Director, his babies being Paul Dixon and Bob Braun and the sponsors of both their television shows.

Mr. McCluskey started out in the world of show business singing Scotch and Irish ballads. George Biggar, then at WLS and later of WLW, hired the genial singer to sing such songs at the Chicago audience WLS had. So Bill moved from Pittsburgh to Chicago where eventually he ended on *The National Barn Dance*. Bill was the one who was the master of ceremonies on the 11 P.M. to midnight portion of the barn dance, telling the listeners out there in radioland, "Good night and God bless you!" But in 1939, Biggar came to WLW—and Bill came along. Their assignment: *The Boone County Jamboree*.

Says Bill McCluskey in recalling the Chicago days before coming to Cincinnati, "I remember when Millie and Dolly and the Girls of the Golden West were invited to appear on *The Fleischmann Yeast Hour* with Rudy Vallee. This was in 1936. The reason I remember so well is that Rudy Vallee paid for a duet but actually got a trio as Millie, who was and still is Mrs. William McCluskey, was pregnant with our oldest boy, Billy."

Biggar and McCluskey were brought to Cincinnati. Why? "You've got to remember," says Mr. McCluskey, "that a few years before, WLW had been operating with 500,000 watts, but that was behind us. Still, as a 50,000-watt clear-channel station, WLW was and is a power to be reckoned with. Mr. Shouse wanted 'goodwill ambassadors' out there on the road, flying the WLW banner. That was the real reason for bringing me in. I was to handle the talent end, getting these country music people out there where they could be seen in all the places WLW reached. I wasn't hired as a singer. I guess he had heard me sing."

The balladeer-turned-talent-booker recalls days and weeks and months of one-night stands in county fairgrounds everywhere. He would have one show out on the road five days, a night here and a night there, bringing it back to the Cincinnati area on weekends for the *Boone County Jamboree*. WLW in those days had country music people the way some barns these days have mice. WLW had enough country music talent to handle all the daily shows broadcast as well as to work the one-night stands out in the countryside. After awhile, said McCluskey, the ones working over the air would trade places with the ones on the road—and thus, both got exposure both ways. He estimates WLW had as many as forty country music people on the staff or on the road—full-time!

In those days the *Boone County Jamboree* featured Lazy Jim Day, Helen Diller the Canadian Cowgirl, Louise Massey and the Westerners, Red and Tige Turner, the Delmore Brothers, and Grandpa Jones—plus others already listed elsewhere. In charge of the WLW Artists Bureau, McCluskey was there the day Biggar pulled his biggest coup: he brought Lulu Belle and Scotty from the *National Barn Dance* to the *Boone County Jamboree*. But most times, Bill wasn't there to enjoy the fruits of WLW's success. Most times he was out there somewhere, comforting and cheering the talent on the one-night stands. Or discovering talent.

He recalls in the mid-forties that "one of the greatest natural performers and still the sweetheart of the (present)

[61]

Hayride joined the show. I am speaking of how Bonnie Lou joined us in 1944. In December of that year Bill Sachs of *Billboard* and I were on an afternoon train to Chicago to cover the International Showman's Convention at the Sherman House. Bill and I were in the club car having a light refreshment when we fell into conversation with a young salesman from Kansas City and naturally we exchanged information about our respective occupations. This gentleman proceeded to rave about a young teen-age country and western singer named Sally Carson who in his opinion was the best in the business and was heard over KMBC, Kansas City. We asked him to get Sally Carson to send a transcription of various songs as well as some pictures. She did and then we asked her to send another recording, singing 'Freight Train Blues,' a number made famous by our old friend Red Foley. She did, we hired her at WLW, changed her name to Bonnie Lou, and she has been with WLW ever since, riding the top of the waves of popularity on the *Midwestern Hayride*."

Why change her name? Says McCluskey, "When it came time for Bonnie to make the decision whether to come to WLW or stay with KMBC, there was a matter of 'rights' to the name Sally Carson because the station 'owned' the name. So she changed her name and joined us during a show at the Midland Theater in Newark, Ohio. Why had I asked for her to record "Freight Train Blues"? Because I wanted a number with a yodel in it. Yodeling was big in those days and in many places it still is. Bonnie Lou is the best in the business."

McCluskey had a hand in bringing Ernie Lee to WLW and the Cincinnati area, too. In those days everyone in the business watched—with wonder—as Burl Ives created a folksong sensation in such posh places as the Palmer House in Chicago where no one had supposed his type of song would please. It was what McCluskey calls a "getaway nightclub act," one that differs from the regular fare offered the tipplers. "So WLW wanted me to get my hands on someone like Burl Ives," McCluskey recalls. "When I went up to Detroit that year for the fair convention, I heard Ernie Lee for the first time. He was no newcomer. He was a star in Detroit in his own right. I made an audition recording of him. When the powers that be at WLW heard it played, they were impressed. One said he sounded like Ives. Another said he sounded like 'Singing Sam.' We agreed he was a beautiful combination of both. So we convinced him to join WLW and the fun we were having down here. He's one of the nicest guys in a business where nice guys are just about everywhere."

George Gobel was one of the youngsters—'way back then—that Bill McCluskey chaperoned around the hayshaker circuits. That was when George would have been too young for his Alice. That was when he was the boy cowboy star of the *National Barn Dance*. He used to stop the shows with his yodeling and his western songs. When WLS decided to "travel" him on its roadshows, George was handed over to McCluskey, then the roadshow emcee, for safekeeping. George was fourteen at the time. Bill was only a dozen years his senior. But Bill proved to be a good chaperone. George did not get into any kind of trouble.

Another under the wing of Bill McCluskey was Doris Day, the one you think she is. She is a Cincinnati local. According to Bill, "To my knowledge she was a dancer, but she broke her leg, so she started vocalizing and became the tremendous talent she is today. But back then, she

[63]

was on one of those one-night-stand circuits with us. It was at the Butler County fairground in Hamilton, Ohio, that she made her first appearance before a fair audience. It was a cold September night and the poor little girl was scared to death. She wasn't used to working a fair grand-stand—and you couldn't blame her. The way the setup is, there are the stands where the people are, there is a big open gap where the track is, and out there almost beyond the *feel* of the audience the performers are. It is not an intimate setting. Some people need intimate settings to perform their best and Doris, at the time, was like that. I can remember her looking at me, nervous as a cat, and she said real low, 'Oh, Bill, the audience is so far away. What'll I do?' I said, 'Doris, you'll sing a darned snappy tune for your opening, it will go over big, and after that you'll sell 'em with a damn sweet one.' And that's what she did. They loved her. And now the whole world does. Well, she's earned the affection of the audiences. They give and she gives. And what they give one another is pretty wonderful."

And, add Andy Williams to the list of those who have been under the wing of WLW and Bill McCluskey. Says McCluskey, "I think it was about in 1940 that their dad brought them in—the Williams Brothers, I mean. The father used to bring them to the studio—and after they finished their singing take them on to school. Andy was about fourteen at the time. And they went off on the one-night county fair circuits with the rest of us. But there were some pretty strict laws about kids that age doing personal appearances so I even had to arrange for a tutor for them while they were on the road. They went on from WLW to national fame and they deserve all the breaks they got. I remember when the two of them were on *Time to Shine*, a program WLW put together for Griffin Shoe Polish. WLW has good orchestras now and it had good ones then, too. There were men like Jimmy James and Jimmy Wilbur. We had a show called *WLW on Parade*, Doris Day sang, and it was wonderful. That played the county fairs, too. We weren't restricted to offering only country music, but there was nothing wrong with country music. You have to understand *that!*"

There are eighty-eight counties in Ohio—and Bill Mc-Cluskey's wandering country minstrels have set foot in most of them. Also, add the nearby counties of Indiana, Kentucky, Michigan, and—even—Pennsylvania. WLW country performers used to do a land-office business each Sunday in the Pennsylvania parks. When not playing fairs, the country performers would play festivals. And on and on and on. But most important, these were *honest* shows that WLW "traveled." Now and then a national headliner will hit the trail of one-night stands, his entourage being simply himself and his wardrobe trunk. The rest of the talent for his show would be "pickup"—that is, local performers and musicians used to fill out the program to make it worth the price of admission. WLW would have none of this. Says McCluskey, "The station kept faith with the listeners who came out in all kinds of weather to see the people they had only heard before on the radio. The people knew they could depend on the shows that WLW would bring to their towns and villages. That made more of them show up. That made our roadshows even that much more successful."

The sheer broadcast *power* of WLW was a powerful force to bring families into the fairgrounds by the carload. Thus, the size of the town where the show played did not matter terribly much. People came from the backroad townships and the hinterlands to share an evening with Lulu Belle and Scotty, their "radio" friends. Bill McCluskey said that all he ever looked for was an auditorium or theater or grandstand big enough to hold the friends the WLW country singers attracted. Consider, for example, Wapakoneta. Now everyone knows where it is because that's where the astronaut Neil Armstrong is from. But Wapo—as some of the natives call it—is not exactly the center of the universe. Yet, when the WLW country singers entertained there each year at the county fair, people thronged, some from as far away as fifty miles! Because the fair manager knew the drawing power of the WLW talent, Harry Kahn who ran the Wapo' event would make Bill McCluskey promise that for six months prior no WLW talent would play within a thirty-mile radius of his county seat.

"In those days," says Bill McCluskey with affection, "before television, the good people out there wanted to see these people they had only heard on the radio. If a show from WLW wasn't coming to their town or village, they would load up the family car and drive as far as seventy-five miles to see their friends. Just as television today takes Paul Dixon and Bob Braun right into the homes, we did almost the same with our roadshows. We couldn't get into all the homes, so we did the next best thing. We held shows everywhere we were wanted—and we were wanted everywhere."

The WLW performers would be booked everywhere. They even went as far west as Danville, Illinois. McCluskey said that used to be a great audience. "But," he adds, "we would not travel too deep into Kentucky because down

[66]

there were so many hillbilly bands that were homegrown right in their own little villages and hollows. We would draw great crowds in Louisville and Lexington, though. About the only areas the hillbillies from WLW missed in Ohio were in the far northeast where Cleveland, Ashtabula and Conneaut are. The troupes would venture as far north, say, as Mansfield, playing a string of local theaters in the area. The WLW group entertained to packed houses in Battlecreek and Jackson, Michigan, too.

Getting there—and back to WLW in time for the Saturday night broadcasts—posed the problems. Mr. McCluskey remembers the worst time the traveling involved them. "It was" he says "when we arranged to have a WLW bus. I was in favor of a bus, too, because until then most of the talent traveled in their own cars arriving at the town we were to play in like stragglers. With the bus I felt we could keep the entire unit intact. We would all arrive at the place at the same time and my nerves would be a little less ragged. But the bus broke down during our busiest summer season and I spent most of that summer getting people on and off of trains and in and out of cars. But we never missed a show. Sometimes I don't see how we made some of them, though.

"I remember one night in particular. It was at the Delaware County Fair. Well, the bus had broken down again so we drifted into town piecemeal. And the university was starting its semester at the same time; the hotel had been unable to hold our reservations; and so there we were—all of us—without a place to stay for the night. Well, I happened to remember I knew a man at the Ringling Brothers Circus which was playing at the fairgrounds, too. So I went out and he was very kind. He let our whole troupe sleep in one of those big circus tents. We spent the night actually

[67]

on the county fairgrounds. There were some crazy moments on the road . . ."

Although now to see WLW stars at the Ohio State Fair in Columbus seems as natural as seeing them on the tube every day, things were not always like that. The first to beef up the state fair attendance figures was the happy crowd from the *Boone County Jamboree*. The WLW show played the Ohio State Fair since 1939 and, says McCluskey, in 1941, in addition to the *Boone County Jamboree*, WLW helped start one of the most ambitious offerings, a show every afternoon and evening throughout the fair's run. "We called it *By Dawn's Early Light.* WLW put it together because the fair officials had come to us with a problem. The officials were tired of the same old circus acts that played in front of the grandstand every year and they wanted something that was different. WLW put me in charge. I hired a producer. I hired Joe Jackson, the Silent Comedian. I hired a ballet team. When I was finished, I had a cast of three hundred. It was a historical extravaganza going from the Civil War to the start of the First World War. And it was a complete WLW production! We stole the thunder from the circus acts. We broke all records for the state fair. It wasn't what you would label broadcasting, but that's the way the powers-that-be are around here. Anything we can do to help the community, we do, whether it concerns broadcasting or not."

When did the *Boone County Jamboree* become the *Midwestern Hayride*—and why? Says Mr. McCluskey, "The name was changed in 1945 because we were after a higher type corn, twenty gallons to the acre. The *Boone County Jamboree*, as such, was more or less a local name and because WLW reached out beyond, we wanted a name that did, too. There was a Broadway show at the time called *Mexican Hayride* and since WLW *is* the great midwest, we added Midwestern and came up with *Midwestern Hayride*. I think it was Mr. Shouse himself who decided on the name. He had just returned from New York on a business trip and one of his visions was midwestern shows to be aired in New York. So he came back with 'hayride', I added 'midwestern' and there you are. When you think of a hayride you think of a horsedrawn wagon, a lot of people sitting up there having fun, a real good get-together. Well, that's the way the *Midwestern Hayride* is."

Shows *can* be overproduced and for a little while in its history, the *Midwestern Hayride was*. "Now," says McCluskey, "I see 'communication' on that show with Kenny Price running it. And they're all having fun, the way a gathering like that should be. Oh, listen, when we used to travel the show and there would be everybody on the stage at the start of the show, those were wonderful days. You would see Lulu Belle and Scotty sitting there with everybody else, nobody left the stage, a spotlight would feature whoever was performing, and when he was through the people on the stage and the people in the audience would *both* applaud. It was everybody, on the stage and in the audience, having a good old-fashioned time. That's how I see the *Midwestern Hayride* becoming more and more. It's getting even better. Don't you think that's beautiful?"

When both the *Boone County Jamboree* and the *Midwestern Hayride* were broadcast from the Ninth and Elm Street studios of WLW, there were—for those behind the scenes—moments of bewilderment. Said a television director just back from Korea, "I'll never forget the first week I directed the show. There I was, at the halfway break in

[69]

the show, and I look out of the control room window to see all the talent pack up their instruments and leave! I didn't know what was going on, if the studio was on fire, or what. Also, since they had all vanished, I didn't know *who* I was going to do the rest of the show with. Nobody told me they were shifting. The ones from television were going down to radio and the ones from radio were coming up to finish the television show. But it worked out somehow. Ernie Lee was doing the show then. Nothing got him excited, but there I was in the control room, looking for the panic button."

In the hinterlands, Bill McCluskey used to have *his* problems, too, like too many in the audience.

"I think it was at Urbana," he says, "and at the county fair. We were scheduled for one performance only. But long before the evening show was to go on for the grandstand, the grandstand was jammed. There wasn't a seat available. Everyone was sitting there, waiting. And still more people were waiting outside to get in. So I said to one of the fair officials, 'Look, do you have any chairs we can put on the track between the stands and the stage so the others out there can get in and see the show, too?' There were no chairs available. We had already used every one, it seems, in the county. That's how big the audience was. 'Okay,' I said, 'Then what about some bales of hay?' And by golly, we got bales of hay, put them on the race track between the grandstand and the stage, and that made everything perfect. We lost that 'gap' between the stage and the audience, the one that had bothered Doris Day years before. From then on, if the fair was big enough, out would come the bales of hay, people would sit on them, and

—listen, they even paid extra because they were considered 'box seats'."

Now, it seems, only the *Midwestern Hayride* remains of all that has gone before. But not really. Bonnie Lou is still boffo. And country music is heard just about everywhere, isn't it, and not just on special programs dedicated to those down there on the farm. Those on the farm have moved to the city, they read *Playboy* or *The New York Times*, and their back-home music is *in*. So WLW hasn't stopped programming country music. Now, on the tube and on the radio, country fare is everywhere, a part of the whole which is the total audience. And those personal appearances of yore? As far as the crowd at WLW, personal appearances are still winners. The fact that viewers can see Bonnie Lou on the tube does not mean that they won't still drive fifty miles to see her in person. Ask her. Ask any of them. The excitement that was radio is now television's too— and that excitement *attracts*. Have you ever seen the Paul Dixon crowd in the mobs at Columbus, Indianapolis, and Dayton? Have you ever seen the hordes who turn out to see Bob Braun in person? And three-hundred pound Kenny Price, a crowd unto himself, attracts another whenever he appears.

"We're lucky at WLW," says Bill McCluskey. "WLW has been in the talent business so long and has so much invested in it that when television came along we had a bigger backlog of talent ready for it than most any other radio station in the country had. When we went on the air in television, we could start right out doing 'live' shows. We didn't have to 'build' them. WLW had already built them. We had built them in theaters around Ohio, at county fairs, at festivals. Thanks to all of those—the Pa and Ma McCormicks and the Lulu Belles and Scotties and the Bonnie Lou's—when television came, WLW was ready. The television 'remotes' we do with Paul Dixon and Bob Braun and the *Midwestern Hayride* are still terrific. There is still standing-room-only. We get thousands of requests for tickets we can't handle. The seating capacity of the auditoriums just isn't there to handle it. The WLW talent still attracts. The personal touch is still there."

The powerful little 5-watter down in Rosedale had grown up.

WLW during the forties?

Well, the times were turbulent and so was the growth of the station. The forties cover that moment before Pearl Harbor when life was reasonably sweet and there was no television to speak of, to that moment when television was here, there, and everywhere—firmly established and Ruth Lyons was selling sets like crazy because everyone wanted to see her on the tube. To capsule the forties is to capsule a generation of kids, now parents and no longer understanding their own kids. Streetcars still ran in Cincinnati during most of the decade and so did the Mount Adams incline that hoisted orange streetcars up the hill and into Eden Park. The forties were the moment of the B-17, the B-29, and the 4-F. Some cars still had running boards. All of the teenagers had bobbysocks. Zoot suits were a passing fashion note. Songs like "Elmer's Tune," "I'll Walk Alone," "Green Eyes," "Juke Box Saturday Night," "On A Slow Boat to China," and "Mairzy Doats" were the order of the decade. Frank Sinatra was coming of age. And, via foxholes and beachheads and USO performers, so were a lot of guys. This was the decade of Pearl Harbor. Where were *you* when the bombs fell there? This was the decade of "lettered" days: D-Day, V-Day, and the rest. Remember Joe Foss? Audie Murphy? Quonset huts? Ration stamps? Rita Hayworth? And the legs of Betty Grable? Bill Mauldin? And the gold stars in the windows? Joe Palooka went to war. So did Dixie Dugan, Smilin' Jack, Tillie the Toiler, and Daddy Warbucks. This was the decade of *Forever Amber*, *Brave Men*, and *The Robe*. Later, there would be Milton Berle and there would be Eden Ahbez who sang about an enchanted boy who touted others on love. This was the decade of Hopalong Cassidy, Ed Gardner's *Duffy's Tavern*, and Truman-vs-Dewey. Add the *Kinsey Report* (wow!) and Gertrude Berg's entrance into television as Molly Goldberg. And the Kaiser—the car, that is—and Howdy Doody Time. *And* Gorgeous George—in the wrestling ring. The look was—of all things—the midi. And the music was from *South Pacific* and *Oklahoma*. This was, simply put, the forties and WLW was there, too, along with about 760 other radio stations.

As the world situation grew gloomier, prior to Pearl Harbor, news commentators filled the airwaves. By turning a dial you could hear such instant authorities as Dorothy Thompson, General Hugh S. Johnson, Fulton Lewis, Jr., H. V. Kaltenborn, Norman Brokenshire, Walter Winchell, Arthur Hale, Elmer Davis, Gabriel Heatter, Boake Carter, Upton Close, John Gunther, Quincy Howe, and Edward R. Murrow. In juxtaposition—as an escape—more and more soap operas founds themselves being broadcast. As the forties began, WLW was operating again with 50,000 watts regularly—no longer the whopping 500,000 watts —but after midnight, as W8XO, into the wee hours, it still beamed out 500,000 experimentally, usually till its 2:30 A.M. signoff. It was, though, authorized to play with the extra power until 6 A.M., but WLW chose not to do that. WLW was always in there, trying to sell the government on how wonderful its 500,000 watt capability was. For instance, in 1939 when Germany invaded Poland, WLW offered to use its 500,000 watts in the daytime so listeners in remote areas might be posted on current events beyond the shadow of the milking shed. Washington said no thanks. However, in 1943, the Office of War Information did ask the FCC to let WLW play with 500,000 watts and more experimentally as W8XO, after midnight only. Tests were conducted on an off-and-on basis. At times, during the tests, run after midnight, WLW, as W8XO, sometimes cranked out as much as 700,000 watts! Some of the engineers were James Rockwell, Floyd Lantzer, William Alberts, and Fritz Leydorf. The powerful transmitter, during the war, had been dismantled for possible shipment to the Mediterranean War Theater—or to Australia. But, says Clyde G. Haehnle, who helped with the crating, it never went anywhere. It just sat in Mason, Ohio. Hurry up, as they say in the military, and wait.

In 1942, Crosley moved closer into the city. He purchased the Elks Temple at Ninth and Elm, where the station is presently, for $200,000. Two years later, 1944, the building was ready for occupancy. This was, of course, during the years of World War II—and things at WLW were not quite normal. Things were not normal *anywhere*. Nearly one-third of all the staff members of WLW went off into the war effort—into either the military itself or government service. And those who stayed home at WLW were just as involved.

In the *Saturday Evening Post* of September 23, 1944, appeared a story about a powerful voice WLW built at Bethany. For those of you who like to collect the trivia of yesteryear, note that the same issue carried an article titled *What the Buzz Bomb Means To You* ("It will revolutionize warfare," said Martin Sommers, then the magazine's science editor) ; contained an explanation of why the magazine was for Governor Dewey ("I believe that President Roosevelt can no longer think straight," said magazine editor Ben Hibbs) ; plus a short story by Clarence Buddington Kelland: *Alias Jane Smith*. But we digress. The article we have in mind is called *The Loudest Voice in the World*. In talking about this powerful transmitting facility, the article's author, Arthur W. Baum, noted that "actually the Bethany station is a dust cloud that we are throwing into the Axis' face in a race in which we started with iron shoes against a fleet-footed opponent already far down the track."

More technically, said Mr. Baum, "The whole operation [at Bethany] is roughly the reverse enlargement of the small radio in the average home. But where the home radio has tubes a fist high, Bethany's 250,000-watt amplifier tubes are a foot and a half high, giants especially built for the first time by Federal Telephone and Radio Corporation. And instead of a scrap of aerial tucked in a box or hung on a roof, Bethany has rhombics anchored 165 feet in the air. Each pole at the four corners of each of these antenna diamonds is made of two telephone poles joined by a collar at the butts and pushed upright by a hundred-foot crane that was pulled down on its face three times before all the poles were up and guyed. Traveling about through the stations are some sixty miles of copper wire . . .

"The antennae and the transmitting station . . . lie behind a rural mailbox which is simply inscribed BETHANY TRANSMITTERS. From the mailbox a short road leads past a barn to a fresh white building and from the building copper pipes and wires lead out across the fields to twenty-four rhombics. All of this together covers about a square mile, and if it looks like anything at all from the air above, it must resemble a great spider with a building for a body and wire legs ending in diamond boxing gloves. From the ground, however, the most powerful shortwave station in the world looks like nothing but a huge complication of tall orange-and-white poles, lateral wires and guy cables. . . . Some of the nearby farmers have decided that whatever the station may be, it is an abominable desecration of a square mile of good corn land."

The gadgetry—all of it—belonged to the Office of War Information. The buildings from which the gadgetry sprouted belonged to the Defense Plant Corporation. But its operation was in the hands of WLW engineers, being the special baby of chief engineer R. J. Rockwell who takes an uncomplicated approach to broadcasting. He feels that to have the "loudest radio voice in the world" is a mere matter of the right tubes, the right power, and the right soldering of this gidget to that gidget. Small wonder he acquired the name Tinkertoy, because, at any given moment on any given problem, he could come up with something to solve the problem, be it the world's most powerful shortwave transmitter abuilding or changing a fuse in the fusebox at home.

[77]

As noted in the article, when this marvelous engineer found himself without a resistance unit needed to test the transmitter's output, he didn't run to the catalog and order a unit that would cost the station several hundred bucks. He went to the nearest hardware store, bought one hundred bathroom heater elements, forty-nine cents each, and connected them in series on a board. Thus, through the bathroom heaters flowed the power that would normally broadcast radio things (a soap opera, a weather report, the voice of a friend) to a half-dozen states. Another of his gadgets: a push-button method of switching radio frequencies via a miniature copper railroad track enabling the transmitter to jump—instantly—from one frequency to another.

"There is," said Mr. Baum in the article, "tremendous dissipation of power in the transmission of shortwave signals. For one thing, only about a third of the electric power put into the job of vibrating the electronic equivalent of a tuning fork and imposing upon the resultant frequency the human voice ever issues from the wires of the sending aerial. Then, in shortwave beamed at North Africa, for example, the signal travels in a series of bounces from the ionosphere to the earth and back again and finally showers on the target area. To reach the targets and to activate the tubes of the radio sets of distant listeners overseas, Bethany's big transmitters will send a hundred quadrillion times as much power as a single receiving set abroad needs to wake it up. That, in turn, means a heavy bundle of energy as it leaves the transmitting antenna. This power cannot be seen or felt or smelled, but sometimes it makes itself evident in curious ways . . ."

True, true. Even before the war when WLW was

[78]

tinkering with 500,000 watts in the standard-band of broadcasting—the 700 on the dial we all know—the engineers had to work out a system of grounding because, as mentioned in the earlier chapters, the power played strange ghostlike tricks on the nearby communities, like never letting some of them turn off their houselights. In addition, barns that sported tin roofs found they had become radio receivers in spite of themselves—and there the barn was, playing the music of *Moon River* to the cows in the field and giving the latest weather report to the birds that flew above. Problem was even greater with the shortwave power and especially broadcasts that would be aired in foreign languages. Ohio farmers are wonderful and sensitive gentlemen all. None of them likes to pass a barn that is jabbering at them in German. But proper grounding solved *that* problem.

Lawrence Lichty was also impressed with the genius of Chief Engineer Rockwell. In his thesis, Mr. Lichty noted that "in January, 1959, an improved transmitter went into operation at WLW. The rebuilding of the WLW transmission facilities cost about $300,000 [this was when most were moaning that radio itself was dead] and was under the direction of R. J. Rockwell, vice president of engineering. With the new facilities, including the Rockwell Cathanode Transmitter, and the new automatic gain control equipment, WLW began broadcasting with a frequency range from below twenty cycles per second to above 20,000 cycles per second with distortion of less than one percent. A microwave relay system was installed to send the WLW signal from the downtown Cincinnati studios to the transmitter at Mason, Ohio. That system operated with the call letters KQK59. With these engineering changes the station management began calling WLW 'The Nation's Highest Fidelity Station.' . . . WLW transmission was tested by the McIntosh Laboratory, Binghamton, New York. According to the report of Frank McIntosh, president, the WLW signal ranged from seventeen to 21,500 cycles per second—more than ten full octaves—with a distortion of 0.3 per cent. Mr. McIntosh stated that: 'it should be recognized that while FM is capable of this same order of fidelity, many stations have not achieved it because of limitations in microphones, preamplifiers, circuits, and program sources.'"

Said the genius Mr. Rockwell himself in *Broadcasting Magazine*, April 13, 1959: "There seems to be a prevailing misconception that AM stations are limited in their permissable band width. (If an AM station used a band only ten kilocycles wide it would transmit sounds only as high as five thousand cycles because of the nature of the amplitude modulation transmission.) Actually, this is not true. The basic allocations system for the AM band was originally set up by the FCC to provide adjacent channel separation of 40 kc in the same area and sufficient geographical separation on the 10, 20 and 30 kc channels to minimize interference. As a result high fidelity transmission *can* be accomplished in the AM band."

If, that is, you've got a chief engineer who is a genius; and *if*, that is, the station is willing to back his dreams with the bucks that make such dreams come true. What can be done in broadcasting is not always what will be done in broadcasting. In every field of endeavor there is usually a standard by which all others in that field are judged. In broadcasting, most outsiders say, WLW *is* the standard.

[80]

A quick capsuled history of WLW during the forties would read this way:

1940: Meteorologist added to the staff, making WLW first station with its own weatherman.

1941: WLW purchases farm from which to operate and broadcast farm programs. Named *Everybody's Farm* and located at Mason, Ohio, it was visited each year by more than 25,000 people. Also that year, WWDC, the Washington radio station Avco was to buy in 1965, was founded.

1944: The Bethany transmitting plant, mentioned earlier in this chapter, went on the air for the *Voice of America*. Also, WLW sold WSAI.

1945: The FCC approved the sales of the Crosley Corporation to the Aviation Corporation (now Avco).

1946: Crosley's experimental TV station, W8XCT, embarked on a regular schedule of telecasting one hour weekly although there were less than a hundred receiving sets in the Cincinnati area.

1947: By the end of this year W8XCT was telecasting twenty hours per week. On September 21, the first baseball broadcast was telecast locally.

1948: WLWT was granted its commercial license. On February 2, the *Golden Gloves Boxing Tournament* became its first sponsored telecast. The station's formal opening was seven days later. In April, WLWT became the first television station to sign an NBC-TV affiliated contract in the nation, but no cable existed to connect the network to the station. Muddy kinescopes were used. On February

13, some say, the *Midwestern Hayride* started on WLWT.

1949: Up in Dayton, Ohio, WLWD went on the air that March 15. Less than a month later, April 3, WLWC went on the air in Columbus. In January of that year, John Murphy joined WLW—January 1, to be exact. In September, Ruth Lyons started on television.

Television began at WLW long before the Japanese had a go at Pearl Harbor. Gordon Waltz, now producer of the Paul Dixon Show, recalls his prewar years in the hire of WLW. He used to go down to a local department store with early television equipment—camera, monitor, cable, and a fistful of flood lamps—to "produce shows" from one part of the store to another. But along came the Japanese, and television, as a gadget, was set aside for the most part. The day the Japanese bombed Pearl Harbor, Gordon Waltz was at the WLW studios, directing *Canal Days* which featured Ray Shannon. Programs that day were interrupted by bulletin after bulletin, but, says Gordon Waltz, "We got through the program as best we could. Then we sat around, becalmed, and talked of war."

So did WLW. It talked war at whoever cranked in 700 on the dial. Three days before Pearl Harbor, December 4, 1941, WLW must have anticipated the upcoming debacle. Katherine "Kit" Fox was appointed "war program director" for both WLW and WSAI, being then one of the more than two hundred in the hire of both stations. The year before that, James C. Fidler had been appointed weatherman for the stations, the first—as noted—meteorologist ever to be in the full-time hire of any commercial broadcaster. During the first few years of the war—1941 to 1944

[82]

—WLW profits dipped. But, said the station, "More advertisers spent more money to sell more merchandise to more people on WLW than any other station in the world." Parse that sentence.

A merchandising department, under the head of "Chick" Allison helped. It was started in June, 1941. But even before that, the station was hot to trot in the areas of merchandising and promotion. And still is, in case any prospective advertisers are tuned in to this paragraph. Anyway, when James D. Shouse and Robert E. Dunville came up river from St. Louis in 1937, they started WLW merchandising and promoting in a big way. Before such things, however good, had been more or less hit-or-miss. In the spring of 1939 WLW had published and distributed a heady pamphlet called *The WLW Plan of Merchandising*. Also, it mailed weekly to eleven thousand wholesalers a newsletter called *Buy-Way*. Market research was conducted by the station in Dayton and Columbus as well as in Cincinnati itself. WLW, with regularity, sent publicity about its programs to as many as three thousand newspapers, radio magazines, and trade magazines that broadcasters and advertisers read. In January, 1941, the station lined up Dr. Richard R. Mead from the University of Pennsylvania who put together a thoughtful report telling would-be advertisers how they could better spend their bucks on WLW to reach 345 midwestern cities—rather than spend it elsewhere, that is. Also the station lined up fifteen hundred housewives to test new products. Marsha Wheeler and Ruth Engemeyer broadcast the findings of this horde over a program called *WLW Consumers' Foundation*. The real point of all this effort? Well, says Lawrence Wilson Lichty in his study, "[it] was to counter the reduction of WLW's power. In 1939 WLW began 'selling results, service, and time, rather than a lot of watts.'" Which, by then, it no longer had.

Also, WLW had just come out of some kind of donnybrook about broadcasting the World Series in 1939. That was the year that the Cincinnati Reds, owned by Powel Crosley, Jr., and guided by Bill McKechnie won the National League pennant aided by such darlings of the diamond as Ernie Lombardi, Bucky Walters, Paul Derringer, and Frank McCormick. The fact that the New York Giants beat them four straight games is neither here nor there. The point is for a while no one was sure who in Cincinnati was going to broadcast the series at all. WLW, then an NBC affiliate, carrying one of the NBC networks, but the other NBC net was divvied up between WCKY and WSAI. In June of that year, WLW agreed to carry enough programs from the NBC "red network" to keep the network officials happy, only along came the World Series which would have been eliminated by this agreement because the series that year was to be broadcast by Mutual, a network that WLW and three other stations had originated in 1934 when everybody and his brother were starting radio networks. Meanwhile, WKRC, then carrying most of the Mutual network programs, was sitting with the possibility of broadcasting a series in which Powel Crosley's team was playing. WLW fussed a little, offered to carry the Mutual broadcast of the series free on WSAI, but Mutual said no thanks—and thus, in 1939, the team owned by the gentleman who also owned WLW had their series efforts broadcast in Cincinnati over a rival outlet. Red Barber, formerly WLW broadcaster, did the play-by-play along with Stan Lomax and

Powel Crosley, Jr., broadcasting in the beginning
Cincinnati Historical Society

Crosley, in knickers, at Mason, Ohio, groundbreaking, 1928
Cincinnati Historical Society

Jack Hendricks broadcasting "color" of a long-ago Reds game
Cincinnati Historical Society

WLW broadcasting early air show   *Cincinnati Historical Society*

Early performers, Emil Hierman and Lydia Dozier, with the boss
Cincinnati Historical Society

Early radio orchestra at WLW   *Cincinnati Historical Society*

Radio frolics at *Pleasant Valley*: DeVore Sisters in white overalls; Joseph
Lucas conducting   *Cincinnati Historical Society*

President Hoover dedicating Ohio River monument; WLW broadcasting
the event   *Cincinnati Historical Society*

Red Barber broadcasting Reds' ball games. L. to R.: Joe Chambers, Red
Barber, Dave Conlon

Fred Thomas and Peter Grant covering the 1940 Republican National
Convention   *Ken Rarich*

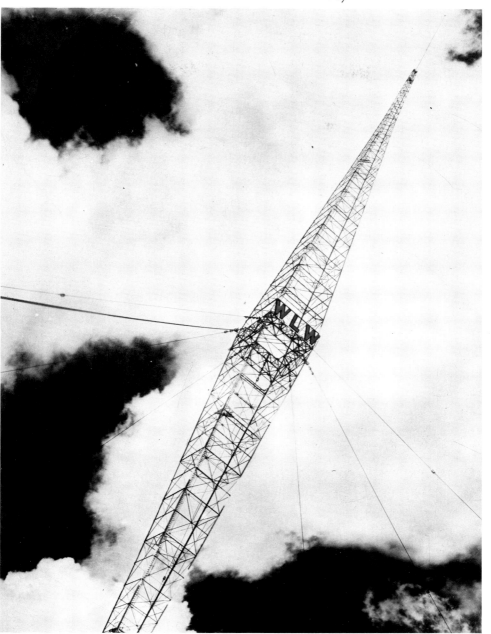

WLW's Tower at Mason, Ohio

Ed Byron who wrote "Moon River" poem, originated *Mr. District Attorney*

Robert E. Dunville . . . who used to run the store   *Ken Rarich*

John Murphy who runs it today . . . and friend   *Robert Metzger*

First radio broadcast over WLW by Ruth Lyons

Ruth Lyons and Jimmy Durante

Ruth Lyons . . . and friend

Ruth Lyons . . . and another friend

Doris Day, then Doris Kappelhoff, at WLW with Jimmy Wilber's Little
Band

The Clooney Sisters, Rosemary and Betty, when singing on *Moon River*

A black and white TV camera from 1949-50

Early days at *Midwestern Hayride*

Midwestern Hayride is now hosted by "the round mound of sound," Kenny Price. Here, Kenny chats with pianist Buddy Ross who has been a member of the *Hayride* cast since the show's inception in 1948

Left to Right: Gene McPherson, Walter Bartlett, and Kenny Price signing on.
Robert Metzger

Reds Manager Sparky Anderson and Bob Braun celebrate Avco's association with the team
Robert Metzger

Bob Elson. And, as noted, the Reds lost in four straight, but don't feel too bad. The next year they were the World's Champions—and *all* Cincinnati celebrated.

Another arrival at the station during the forties was Rosemary Clooney. Along with her sister Betty, she began getting entwined in the hair of night via *Moon River* around 1945 when there was this war going on. Recalls Rosemary, "Happy Lee was organist on *Moon River* and she practically adopted Betty and me. Bless her, she was the only fun we had in those days. We would go to her apartment and Happy and her friend Dick Nesbitt would say, 'Let's take the kids across the river to see a nightclub show.' Little did we know that our first nightclub engagement years later, was to be in one of those clubs—Glenn Rendezvous . . ."

Nick Clooney, the small-fry brother, entered radio and broadcasting via the coffeepot circuit, little stations out in the boondocks. Then he was on the air in Lexington, Kentucky; then in the sixties came to Cincinnati at WLW-Television where he took over most of the chores from Bob Braun when Bob was moved into the *50/50 Club* as permanent host. For a short while, Nick did a show with WLWC in Columbus—and is now with WCPO-TV in Cincinnati, doing just fine, thank you, but let us go gently back to the forties when Nick was little more than a charming urchin doing urchin things in Maysville, Kentucky.

During the war years—and the moments of the forties just prior—WLW news, which had been good before, became even better. As noted elsewhere, network commentators were just about everywhere on the dial. Radio had experts the way late night talk shows now have

[85]

commercials. But, said the late Howard Chamberlain, then program director, "About eighty-five percent of the news broadcast from WLW was prepared at the station itself. We did not rip-and-read, [that is, yank ten feet of news from the news machine and read whatever the teletype had clickety-clicked out to the world] rather, it was all re-written." The WLW news staff during the war years grew from six to fourteen. It had shirt-sleeve newsmen working behind the scenes, adding true professionalism to the on-the-air newscasters. WLW, then, had five commentators of its own, eight rewrite men, and a news editor.

Bill McCluskey recalls those war days, "a big part of our job was entertaining at army camps and hospitals. We visited everywhere with all sorts of talent. I can remember the hospital in Cambridge, Ohio; the fort in Indianapolis; Fort Hayes in Columbus; and a hospital around Danville, Kentucky, where we entertained nurses and prisoners of war from Bataan. There was Camp Atterbury. There were so many of them—and we visited them all. Free, too. This was done as a public service by WLW. We even toured with newsmen. Howard Chamberlain—bless his soul!—was the moderator and we had people like Gregory Zeimer and General Edmunds and Peter Grant—oh, we had them all out there. The news people would do the same things they did on the air, but with questions from the audience. Our news panel visited chambers of commerce, Elks Clubs, Rotary Clubs, Kiwanis Clubs. They would get into timely discussions. There was also a guy named Jim Cassidy who was in our publicity department. After he came back from Anzio beach, he was wanted everywhere to speak . . ."

Howard Chamberlain has finally left his microphone chores at WLW. God whispered the final cue—and that was that. But Howard Chamberlain was, in many ways, a beautiful and lonely tradition around the studios. There is a tide, they say, in the affairs of men; and in the beginning, at WLW, Howard Chamberlain was a part of that wonderful tide. His voice and his charm were as familiar to the midwest as a night train whistling for a forsaken country crossing.

Just before his death, I sat in with Howard Chamberlain and we talked about everything under the sun. He was a gentle and a thoughtful man. Outside he was dignity. There was in him both the imp and the impossible. Was he happy? I do not presume to judge. All I know is, he was good, and whatever he did, he did well. More than that you can't ask of a person.

Then there were soap operas.

We each had our favorites, most of the favorites were humorless (there weren't many laughs in soap operas; there were hardly any smiles; but everyone wept a lot), but my favorite was *Vic and Sade* which wasn't really a soap opera. No one got into deep trouble, no one got into anything, though once in a while Ruthie Stembottom got into Yamelton's Department Store in time for the washrag sale and Uncle Fletcher got into the lobby of the Bright Kentucky Hotel when he wasn't at the depot, watching the trains go by. The characters were Vic and Sade and their son Rush Gook. Later Uncle Fletcher was added, but none of the other characters were ever on the air. The other characters were just talked about by the Gooks, usually on their front porch in that "little house halfway up the next block." Paul Rhymer wrote *Vic and Sade*. There were so many characters talked about. There was Jake Gumpox, the garbageman; the Brick-Mush Man;

Smelly Clark; Blue-Tooth Johnson; Mr. Buller; Ishigan Fishigan of Sishigan, Michigan; and Robert and Slobbert Hink. I take something back. Toward the end of the series other characters *did* appear on the air: Dottie Brainfeeble, Chuck Brainfeeble, and a nephew named Russell Miller. When Vic and Sade's theme, "Chanson Bohemienne," was heard in our home, all conversation stopped for fifteen solid minutes. Beautiful, beautiful memories. It is sad to think that Rush Gook now would be an old man. Only on the other hand, he is probably the same age. People just didn't age in afternoon or morning soap operas. Time hardly moved at all. Yet, time finally caught up with every one of them, and now they aren't any more.

Ma Perkins, as noted elsewhere, originated in Cincinnati at WLW, then went on to the big network centers. But always she came at you, via magic, from mythical Rushville Center where she ran a lumberyard. She didn't always come at you, though, on WLW. WLW was NBC and she moved her village and lumberyard to CBS. In the sixties, long after most soaps had bitten the dust, Ma Perkins threw in the towel, too. Who remembers that last broadcast when Virginia Payne, with twenty-seven years as Ma Perkins under her belt, signed off by saying, "This is our broadcast number 7,065. I first came here on December 4, 1933. Thank you for all being so loyal to us these twenty-seven years. The part of Willie (Fitz) has been played right from the beginning by Murray Forbes. Shuffle (Shober) was played for twenty-five years by Charles Egleston, and for the last two years by Edwin Wolfe who was also our director. The Fay (Perkins Henderson) you've been hearing these past few years has been Margaret Draper; and the part was played for many years by Rita Ascot. For fifteen

[88]

years, Evey (Perkins Fitz) has been Kay Campbell. Helen Lewis plays Gladys (Pendleton) ; and Tom Wells has been played by both John Larkin and Casey Allen. Our announcer is Dan Donaldson. Our writer for more than twenty years has been Orin Tovrov. Ma Perkins has always been played by me, Virginia Payne. If you care to write to me, Ma Perkins, I'll try to answer you. Goodbye and may God bless you . . ."

She left out a few names which is reasonable because there were many through the years of tending the lumber yard and the ids of those who popped into Rushville Center. To give you the *range*—and perhaps to trigger your memory with names you might remember—here, from *Radio's Golden Age*,* by Frank Buxton and Bill Owen (a book you should have if you dig radio things!) is a list of characters who *have* appeared in Rushville Center since time (and Ma Perkins) began.

Ma Perkins . . . . Virginia Payne
Fay Perkins Henderson . . . . . . Rita Ascot, Marjorie Hannan, and Cheer Brentson
John Perkins . . . . Gilbert Faust
Shuffle Shober . . . . Charles Egleston, Edwin Wolfe
Willie Fitz . . . . Murray Forbes
Junior Fitz . . . . Cecil Roy, Arthur Young, and Bobby Ellis
Mr. Farnum . . . . Ray Largay
Mrs. Farnum . . . . Constance Crowder
Zenith Sambrini . . . . Fran Carlon
Greta, the maid . . . . Cheer Brentson
Evey Perkins Fitz . . . . Dora Johnson, Laurette Fillbrandt, and Kay Campbell

---

* *Radio's Golden Age*, by Frank Buxton and Bill Owen, Easton Valley Press, Ansonia Station, N.Y., 1966.

Catherine Shaughnessey.....Cheer Brentson
Josie ....Louise Fitch
Dora ....Mary Frances Desmond
C. Pemberton Toohey.......Fred Howard, Forrest Lewis
Walter Payne..............Curtis Roberts
Miss Adams...............Mary Marren Rees
Dr. Stevens...............Curtis Roberts
Gary St. Denis.............Rene Gekiere
John Adam Drayton........Duke Watson
Frank Fenton..............Barry Drew, Dan Sutter
Mr. Silvus.................Stuart McIntosh
Anton Julikak..............Don Gallagher
Burton Wiley..............Les Tremayne
Sonny Hallet..............Billy Rose
Tommy Taylor............Dolph Nelson
Lyla ....Nanette Sargent
Russell ....Barry Drew
Mr. Mortimer.............Stanley Waxman
Judge Hartley.............Billy Lee, Earl George
Mr. Erp..................Glen Ransom
Eb Martin................Clare Baum
Roger Fritzsimmons.......Jack Samuelson
Zeke Hammill.............Stanley Gordon
Mark Matthews...........DeWitt McBride
Deborah Matthews.........Betty Hanna
Susie Parker...............Sylvia Leigh
Charley Brown............Ray Suber
Dr. Glassman.............Carl Kroenke
Doris Fairchild.............Kay Campbell
Timothy Gallagher.........Forrest Lewis
Jessica Herringbone........Beryl Vaughn
Flossie Herringbone........Angela Orr
Tweetsie Herringbone.......Elmira Roessier
Phineas Herringbone........Herbert Butterfield
Mrs. Pendleton.............Margaret Fuller
Bessie Flounce.............Cecil Roy
Burt Carlon................Jack Petruzzi

Gary Curtis	Rye Billsbury
Augustus Pendelton	Maurice Copeland
Paulette Henderson	Nanette Sargent, Judith Lockser
Stella Carlon Curtis	Marilou Neumayer
Gladys Pendleton	Patricia Dunlap
Mr. Garrett	Wilms Herbert
Joseph	Joe Helgeson
Dr. Andrew White	Casey Allen
Hunkins	Murray Forbes
Gregory Ivanoff	McKay Morris
Rufus	Forrest Lewis
Sam Grim	Charles Egleston
Esther	Lillian White

Paul Dixon used to dig soap operas, too. In his book, *Paul Baby*, he wrote, ". . . because I was hooked (on radio) I listened to everything radio had to offer. I listened, for example, to *Amanda of Honeymoon Hill*. The soap opera used to start with the announcer saying, 'The story of love and marriage in America's romantic South . . . the story of Amanda and Edward Leighton.' When the soap opera first went on the air, the announcer used to say, '*Amanda of Honeymoon Hill* . . . laid in a world few Americans know.' They changed that introduction *fast!*"

Soap operas, if they can be called such, that are on television these days are a different breed of cat. Time is as slow motion in soap operaland as ever, a man saying goodbye in Friday's episode is still departing the following Wednesday, but the problems these days are a bit frothier. None of them would approach that family outing called *Who's Afraid of Virginia Woolf?* but compared to the drama that radio used to crank out to the housewives back then, the televised soap opera is heady stuff, indeed. People *drink* in televised soap operas, but back in the forties all the man ever got was a glass of ice water. In one episode of *Young*

[91]

Doctor Malone, for instance, a man wanted to smoke a cigar and was asked by the heroine, "Don't you want a nice, cold glass of ice water?" Putting away his cigar, the caller said, "Splendid!" And she came back with "How many cubes?" "Two, thank you," he said. So went the orgies back in the forties.

With the exception of Amanda being laid in the deep south, via *Honeymon Hill*, and *Our Gal Sunday* being laid in Virginia, the listeners were never quite sure in which state they might find the soap opera settings of Hartville, Dickston, Simpsonville, Three Oak, Great Falls, Beauregard, Elmwood, Oakdale, Rushville Center, and Homeville. As for me, I always thought Vic and Sade and Rush lived at 1301 Lexington Avenue in Indianapolis because *I* used to live there as a small child, but I'm sure, if you are a *Vic and Sade* fan, you put them up some other block in some other town miles away. The average sequence in soap operas ran about eight weeks, never quite ending, because another sequence would be interwoven into the fabric of the plot before Ma Perkins could sneak out behind the lumberyard for a quick belt to relieve her frazzled nerves. A study of soap operas shows that most villains were city slickers, women who wore lipstick in the morning, and rich men—the more despicable, the better. But none of them proved any match for the soap opera heroines. Goodness always triumphed.

People got sick in soap opera episodes, but their illnesses were not the run-of-the-mill head colds. Most of the time, a character started with a headache, next got dizzy spells, and after that—as any soap opera fan knew from the obvious symptoms—came temporary blindness. They said such a condition would last about two months, after which the patient regained his or her sight, or got a brain tumor and died. Also, in the radio soap operas of the forties there was a lot of amnesia going around. And paralysis of the legs which seemed restricted to males but, like the blindness, could, if the script said so, be temporary. According to James Thurber's delightful study of the subject, "The children of the soap towns are subject to pneumonia and strange fevers, during which their temperatures run to 105 or 106. Several youngsters are killed every year in automobile accidents or die of mysterious illnesses. . . There are a number of Soapland ailments that are never named or are vaguely identified by the doctors as 'island fever' or 'mountain rash.' . . . At least three Ivorytown and Rinsoville doctors are baffled for several months every year by strange seizures and unique symptoms."

Soap opera actors came in all shapes and sizes which was all right because nobody saw them anyway. I personally was in love with Pepper Young's sister Peggy, or at least was in love with her voice, which was the property of Elizabeth Wragge who played the role—but nothing came of that affair. Martin Block was one of the announcers on that program. The Young family lived in Elmwood but they never said where Elmwood was. The program started out as Red Davis, changed its name to Forever Young, and finally became Pepper Young's Family, Elizabeth Wragge being there through all the changes. Many, though, are the tales about the soap opera actors. There was the actor who had the line, "I am Sioux. I make no peace with the Chippewa." But stage fright nailed him to silence and another actor, waiting for his cue, could stand it no more. He bellowed out, "You're Sioux, you big goddam ham; you make no peace with the goddam Chippewa."

[93]

The beautiful forties—allowing, of course, for the sadness and the reality of war. During the war, WLW was, as suggested, involved in shortwave. Lawrence Wilson Lichty reported in his thesis that, "In the fall of 1942 arrangements were made for program materials to be shortwaved to WLW from overseas. The first arrangements were made with the British Broadcasting Corporation and the first shortwave broadcast heard on WLW was an Easter sermon delivered by an English pastor directed at midwestern audiences. This was heard on *Church by the Side of the Road*, a regular WLW program. Rather than send entire programs, usually small segments were recorded for insertion in the WLW shows. . . . For example, information on the role of British women in the war was included in the *WLW Consumers' Foundation* program. Information prepared for use on Gregor Ziemer's news commentary program would begin with, 'Hello, Gregor Ziemer, this is . . . speaking from London, England.' Segments on farming and the life of the farmer in war-torn countries were included in *Truly American, Everybody's Farm*, and *Everybody's Choretime* . . . Later WLW arranged shortwave reports from China, USSR, Switzerland, Turkey, Sweden, Australia, and Canada."

The idea that station management operated with during the war was simple: prior to the war the midwest—WLW-land—had been rather isolated and was, it seemed, of an isolationist mind. The management felt by bringing local touches directly to such people—via the personalized shortwave broadcasts aimed at the midwesterner, plus other things like *Camp Wolters Calling*, and *Your Son At War*—a good public service would result. There was no profit in any of this. In some facets, the operations were such that

[94]

managers got sour looks from the bookkeepers, but a broadcasting service to its managers was something more than a profit-making device. It was, they felt, a proper influence on the community and thus they tossed dollars into the pot to further that premise.

World Front, which was born the same day the Japanese bombed Pearl Harbor, is a good example. The first program on that remembered day consisted of newsmen, announcers, and whatever guests were available, sitting about a WLW microphone trying to add reality to what seemed the unreality of the day. The weekly panel gradually evolved, the most frequent members being such erudite gentlemen as Major General James E. Edmonds; radio commentator Milton Chase; newspaperman William H. Hessler who was foreign news analyst of the Cincinnati *Enquirer*; Joseph Sagmaster who was director of broadcasting for the University of Cincinnati; and *Cincinnati Post* editor Carl Groat. Howard Chamberlain was the moderator—and some of this group was shipped about the midwest by Bill McCluskey in the form of educational one-night stands as mentioned earlier.

By the time the forties ended, WLW-Radio wasn't shipping too many radio programs to the network. At the beginning of the forties though, actually the 1939-1940 broadcast season, many network originations came from the WLW studios. A quick once-over of a few of them: Red Skelton's *Avalon Time*; Bugler Tobacco's *Plantation Party* which had people like Red Skelton, Red Foley, Del King, Whitey Ford (really the "Duke of Paducah"), The Girl of the Golden West, and Peter Grant; Smilin' Ed McConnell; Dorothy Davis, later known as Jeanette Davis; plus the orchestras of Dr. Frank Simon, William Stoess,

Phil Davis, and Virginio Marucci. But the trend was to the "big" production centers. Already *Ma Perkins* had moved her lumberyard elsewhere. *Famous Jury Trials* had a change of venue. Gone were the *Mad Hatterfields* and gone was *Mary Sothern*. The network centers became the network centers. WLW decided to concentrate on its own listening —and later, viewing—area. The emphasis was—and is— on regional programming.

Then the war was over, there was that thing called television, and there we were, sitting in whatever neighborhood tavern sported a television set, watching the wonders of the test pattern.

To those who put together financial reports filled with heady words like *profit* and *loss* and *common stocks* and *debentures*, may we suggest you gloss over this fast. This will be about the *business* side of that thing Powel Crosley, Jr., started. But it will not presume to be the sort of writing that gets mash notes from *Fortune* magazine. Only Rod Serling, who wrote *Patterns*, attempted to get into the inner workings of corporate life. All we can do is view it from the outside with wonder, bewilderment, and affection. Questions like where did Avco come from will be answered in this chapter and, with any luck at all, answered poorly. This book isn't a prospectus touting investment possibilities. It is simply one man's highly casual view of Big Business. Also, I happen to be fond of Crosley—the man, the radio, the refrigerator called Shelvador, and upon occasion, the *car*. Our first electric ice box was a Crosley Shelvador. So do not expect me to be dispassionate and unbiased when I sing the praises of same. The damned thing made ice cubes and later in its career, funny noises. This was not the result of the product. This was the result of my slamming the door a lot, causing everything on the door shelves to rattle. I *think* that was the cause. Mechanical things are lost upon me. They were lost upon the car that Crosley made, too, but we'll get to that in a moment.

Let us follow the corporate bouncing ball carefully.

As I was putting this book together, there appeared in Mary Wood's column in the *Cincinnati Post & Times-Star* a thoughtful letter from a Joseph H. Schoenberger, then in Florida in beautiful Gulfport, commenting where and when WLW actually originated. He thought it originated with the Precision Instrument Company but my research, casual as most of my research is, seemed to prove otherwise. I wrote to Mary to explain my research, stating that "he [Mr. Schoenberger] may very well be right but my research led me down a different path. The radio station that the Precision Instrument Company operated, according to my sources, was WMH, originally 8XB, which had been operating since 1919. Its original antenna was a vertical steel rod and the insulator at its base was an empty wine bottle. Powel Crosley's original station, 8XY—and not 8CR as station promotion would have us believe— first broadcast July, 1921. Later as 8XAA it broadcast from August 1921 until March 1922, when its WLW call letters were established. Crosley later bought out the Precision Instrument Company to acquire the original WMH in the transaction, but this original WMH was an earlier WMH, not the later WMH, forerunner of WKRC and Skipper Ryle. I will not exactly swear to any of this at the moment because I spilled coffee on my notes covering this period

[98]

of WLW's history. Anyway, my notes at this point can't be trusted. One of them, Mary, has you as one of the original cast of *Clara, Lu and 'Em* whereas we all know you got your start in broadcasting with the *A&P Gypsies*, a combo which featured Mort Watters on C-melody sax, John Murphy on drums (that had a light inside and a palm tree painted on the front), and you—with battery-operated pom-poms, you being the DeVore Sisters, all of them. Other than that, everything here in Oxford goes well." Mary never answered my letter. In fact, she took it upon herself to cancel my subscription to her newspaper, and I point these items out to show my study of the business side of Crosley and Avco leaves much to be desired. But there we are, with WLW on the air, and there is Powel Crosley, Jr., with irons in other fires. One final aside: I have toiled for years in the hire of advertising agencies but never once have I been called upon to write an annual report, the companies taking these dreary publications rather seriously. Consider this, then, a report on Avco Broadcasting, nee Crosley Broadcasting, and here we go.

It was in the thirties that Crosley got rolling in manufacturing everything but the kitchen sink. In 1930, for example, he brought out the "Roamio." This was the forerunner of car radios today but it was a monster of a setup: in addition to operating off the A battery the car had, the radio also needed a fistful of others (B and C and D batteries) tucked under the backseat. But the thing sold for $75. And on a clear day, you could hear forever, or as long as the batteries held up.

But while the announcers were announcing things over the WLW microphones out on Arlington Street, Mr.

Crosley himself was sometimes busy in his office, listening to whichever inventor presented himself. Crosley, a natural-born tinkerer, had a natural-born love for fellow inventors just as those who read *Popular Mechanics* seem to belong to a secret and exclusive club. Some of the inventors had invented farfetched things, but Crosley listened to them all. One who wandered in one afternoon in 1931 had an idea that wasn't so farfetched. His premise: if you build a refrigerator with shelves on the door, things could be stored on the door as well as on the shelves of the refrigerator inside. This doesn't seem so startling today, but back then no one had thought of it—except, that is, the man sitting in Mr. Crosley's office, expounding his door-shelf dream.

The idea made sense to Mr. Crosley. He offered the inventor 25¢ royalty on each refrigerator sold that used the inventor's idea, but inventors are ever thus: he held out instead for $15,000 cash which Crosley forked over. The refrigerator, called the Crosley Shelvador, tooted along the production line and hit the streets in 1932 with a hundred dollar price tag. This was about $50 under other refrigerators on the market. Just as he had done with his radio receiving sets, Crosley cranked out the Shelvador as a luxury priced refrigerator so the average man could have ice cubes in whatever he was drinking, Prohibition then being the law of the land. A year after the Shelvador hit the streets for a hundred dollars, it was selling so well Mr. Crosley had five hundred people putting the gadgets together in his Arlington Street factory. Three shifts worked 'round the clock to supply the demand. Said *The New York Times*, Crosley had in less than a year's time almost a million dollars in unfilled orders. Had the inventor accepted the 25¢ royalty instead of the $15,000 cash, he would have been a lot richer. All he ended up was a lot wiser.

While Hink and Dink were chugging from Oxford to the Arlington Street studios to do their blackface bits (à la Amos 'n' Andy; and let us not quarrel which pair was first) other toilers in the Crosley plant were toiling over a variety of things. For instance, a bunch of workers were putting together the Crosley "Go-Bi-Bi," listed as a combination tricycle and baby car and baby talk. Then there was the "Auto Gym" which was an electric vibrator. Then there was the "Icyball," a portable refrigerator. If that doesn't warm, or frost, the cockles of your heart as we stroll down memory lane, Crosley was also cranking out "Peptikai," a pharmaceutical product, and "Koolrest," an air-conditioner he designed himself, and "Tredcote," a tire patch. Add to the list "Driklenit," an auto polish, and "X-er-vac," a scalp massage device, and you can see why Arlington Street with Mr. Crosley there truly swung. To fill in the spare hours he didn't have, in 1934 he bought a piece of the action of the Cincinnati Reds, became president of the baseball club, and two years later bought controlling interest in the Cincinnati nine. That year, 1936, under Chuck Dressen, his team won seventy-four games which would have been grand, but they also lost eighty games. No matter. Good old Ernie Lombardi was in there catching. He, alone, was worth the price of admission. Paul Derringer, that year, struck out 121 batters.

Then, as noted, there was the Crosley car.

In April, 1939, the Crosley Corporation (having changed its name from the Crosley Radio Corporation the autumn before) told the world that Mr. Crosley was going to have another crack at his dream of becoming an automobile-maker. The car, said the announcements, would be called the Crosley (of course). A headline in *The New York Times*, April 29, 1939, said:

$325 Car Set To Go 50 Miles Per Fuel Gallon;
Crosley Puts Its Speed At 50 Miles An Hour.

Crosley said, "I've always wanted to build a practical car that would not only operate at a low cost, but would also sell at a low price. I've been dreaming of this car for twenty-eight years."

But distributors were not exactly beating his door down for distributorships to peddle his two-cylinder gadget. Crosley, forever the free spirit, refused to be either dismayed or stopped. When the cars finally became available in 1939, he tried to sell them through—of all places!—department stores. Plus other established retail outlets. The first models could be seen in the windows of Macy's in New York; and if Macy sold many of them, it didn't tell Gimbels.

World War II pulled the rug temporarily out from under his car dream, but by September of 1944, the war drawing to a conclusion, Mr. Crosley dusted off his dream and started all over again. He estimated he could peddle about 150,000 of them when the war was over and servicemen, wearing ruptured ducks, came home to eat blueberry pie. The postwar engine was not the same as the prewar engine. Much had been learned by industry from the war. Californian Lloyd M. Taylor designed the motor so that it could be constructed from sheet metal. The 26 horsepower puddle-jumper's engine then consisted of 120 steel stampings, tube sections crimped together, and copper brazed into a single unit. All weighed only 138 pounds. The body weighed in at 1000 pounds. Marion, Indiana, was selected as the manufacturing site, and production began. Because some questioned the ability of a small car to contain comfortably an oversized human being, Powel Crosley himself used to shovel his six foot, four inches into the thing. When orders for his little car began to come in, it is said that he was as excited as a little boy. Well, he should have been. He had earned the right, hadn't he?

Reports Lawrence Wilson Lichty, "He (Crosley) was so anxious to get the new cars out that the first five thousand were produced before anyone noticed that the nameplate *Crosley* had been left off. The name on these first cars then had to be painted on the bumper in three-inch high letters."

At the end of the first official sales year (July 31, 1947), more than sixteen thousand of the little cars had been sold at $888 each, and Crosley Motors showed a profit of $476,-065. The next year, thirty thousand more of the little things were sold. When the Korean War came along, materials got harder to come by, though. Labor costs had risen. The handwriting was on the wall. In 1951 Crosley produced about four thousand cars. In 1952 Crosley produced less than two thousand. After losing about a million dollars a year for three years, in 1952 Mr. Crosley closed the plant in Marion, Indiana, and thus slowly died the dream. The company was sold to General Tire for just $60,000 and that, sorry to say, was that. Crosley pottered around at loose ends for nine years—sometimes on his farms (one in Indiana, one in Georgia), sometimes in his homes (one in Cincinnati, one in South Carolina, one in Canada), or on his yacht or traveling with his Cincinnati Reds. On March 28, 1961, Powel Crosley, Jr., died. Yet, even today, on rare occasions, one can see that little car tooting along the streets or over a country backroad. The cars that remain are showing their age and soon they, too, will chug their last chug. They were never beautiful, that must be understood, but Mr. Crosley's dream was. *That*, also, must be understood.

Others had been operating WLW while Mr. Crosley was involved with his dream. By 1945, Crosley had all but severed his connection with the station he fathered. In 1945, Victor Emanuel of the Aviation Corporation signed the papers that made the Crosley Corporation a subsidiary of the Aviation Corporation (now Avco). The Aviation Corporation was born March 1, 1929—a bad year, really, for any company to pop out of the nursery—as part of another car-maker's dream. The Aviation Corporation was one segment of the holdings of E. L. Cord (remember the beautiful, beautiful *Cord* autos?) who made the cars and also tinkered in real estate. His base was Los Angeles, but his companies—of which Aviation Corporation was only one—were, as *Business Week* magazine said, "A hodge-podge." In 1937, according to *Fortune* magazine, the Securities and Exchange Commission had requested that Mr. Cord retire from stock market speculation. Another was American Airways. In 1937, however, Victor Emanuel took over the operation and quietly and calmly made fiscal sense out of what had been rather casual. Victor Emanuel had already earned his credits as a genius in the field of business. Listen, any guy who can take over a utility company from his father and turn it into a sound financial empire of fourteen diverse and successful companies, sell the whole shooting match to Samuel Insull, and retire himself at the age of twenty-eight has to have a lot on the ball. If anyone could make sense of the Aviation Corporation thing, he could and he did. For the record, when you're in the mood to drop a name, *this* Victor Emanuel is no relation whatsoever to those Italian kings, Victor Emmanuel II and III.

The same year, 1945, the Aviation Corporation bought WLW, it bought other things, too: the New Idea Company; the American Central Manufacturing Corporation, and Consolidated Aircraft. In 1947 the name of the company was changed to the Avco Manufacturing Corporation. One of its divisions was the wholly-owned subsidiary the Crosley Broadcasting Corporation, now Avco Broadcasting. If you like to look a little deeper (not much more, please, because some of us are dozing) note that its Lycoming Division in Stratford, Connecticut, made military aircraft engines for the Korean War; while in Cincinnati the (then) Crosley Division made radar and other electronic equipment as well as aircraft structures. Its Avco Everett Research Laboratory in Massachusetts plays around with high-temperature gas dynamics and down there in Nashville, Tennessee, its Avco Aerostructures Division plays around with space-ships like Buck Rogers used to use. Avco also works with missile defense systems as well as a bunch of nondefense things. Its dollars, via the Avco Financial Services, lend cash to us poor folk as well as companies. Marine gas turbine engines are on the menu at its Lycoming Division plant in Stratford, Connecticut. We can only suggest that Avco is much more than Frank Pierce telling us about an approaching cumulus cloud. James R. Kerr now leads the whole shooting match as president and chief executive officer of Avco Corporation and chairman of the board of Avco Broadcasting Corporation. Kendrick Wilson is chairman of the board of Avco Corporation itself. Avco has come a long way since the days of Mr. Cord and his most beautiful automobile. So much for making the members of the board pleased. On to the matter of WLW.

Both the corporate entity and the people who comprise it give back to the communities as much or more than can be seen in any profit and loss statement. A few examples? Okay, there's the Ruth Lyons Christmas Fund, but most of you are aware of that. There are, in addition, all the free public service announcements the stations air. One year the Avco stations figured they had donated more than $7,000,000 to public service institutes for free air-time advertising. That's a hefty budget. And there, up on that hill overlooking downtown Cincinnati, is what is called Mount Olympus: a complete facility, studios, control rooms, rest rooms, tower, the works, equal to most television stations and better than many. Avco rents the whole shooting match to educational station WCET for a buck a year. As the result, WCET can reach over four hundred schools in the area and millions of homes. *Sesame Street* may not be telecast over WLWT, but as the result of Avco-donated facilities, WCET can lay *Sesame Street* on us. For another buck a year Avco rents FM transmitting facilities to the University of Cincinnati. WLW's weather radar installation is part of the U.S. Weather Bureau's severe warning system—and it doesn't cost us taxpayers a dime. Robert Goosman, senior vice president and treasurer of Avco Broadcasting, calmly manages the complicated job of keeping everything straight.

But this sense of public service did not blossom of itself. Some of it came from Powel Crosley. Some of it came from those two gents who came upstream from St. Louis: Robert Dunville and James Shouse. James Shouse arrived in Cincinnati on November 19, 1937, to become general manager

[106]

of WLW-WSAI. He had been general manager of KMOX, St. Louis. Before that, he had been with WBBM, Chicago, and before that, *Liberty* magazine. Dunville, Shouse's assistant in St. Louis, came here a month later to become assistant general manager of WLW as well as manager of WSAI. When, in 1939, WSAI and WLW separated their staffs, Dunville was named WLW commercial manager. It was Shouse's influence that enhanced the public service attitude of the (then) Crosley stations.

"When Jimmy Shouse came from St. Louis radio to take over the management of WLW and WSAI," Mary Wood wrote of her good friend, "he began to change the whole picture of local broadcasting. It was Jimmy's feeling that a radio station had a definite responsibility to the community in which it operated, and to that end he began to build a new public service image for the two Crosley stations.

"To Jim, public service meant serving the public, not just racking up points with the FCC. He hired responsible reporters to cover the news and write it. He was also the first to point up and dramatize local issues with radio documentaries, which won award after award for WLW. During the lean years of the thirties and forties, Shouse gave WLW's support to Cincinnati's Symphony Orchestra and its Summer Opera, along with any other cultural effort which could benefit the community. And during the war years, Crosley's powerful shortwave broadcasting facilities at Bethany were invaluable to our government.

"When television came along, Jim was the first to envision a group of midwestern Crosley TV channels which could cover the same territory which had been served by

[107]

WLW-Radio for so many years. He also believed in building local talent and programming which has resulted in the enduring programs of the *50/50 Club*, *Midwestern Hayride*, and *The Paul Dixon Show* on channel five.

"Jim Shouse was one of the most brilliant men in the broadcasting industry. He was also a rather shy guy with a quick, dry wit and a fey sense of humor who always insisted he was a sucker for a con man. One of his favorite stories concerned an old friend who had, over the years, managed to fast-talk Jimmy into lending him considerable money which was never paid back.

" 'I finally got mad and sued Brad for the last $500 he borrowed from me,' said Jimmy. 'We went to court and I got the judgment.'

"As Jimmy was leaving the courtroom, Brad came up to him, enveloped him in a great bear hug and suggested they repair to the nearest bar so that Brad could buy him a drink and let bygones be bygones.

" 'To my eternal regret, I accepted Brad's invitation,' laughed Jimmy. 'Before we parted, I had not only paid for the drinks but had been persuaded to lend Brad $500 more.'

"Jimmy was an idealist who contributed much to the broadcasting industry. He came a long way from St. Louis . . ."

So, listen, will you, with your eyes, to a program broadcast over WLW on Wednesday, August 25, 1965. You'll hear Jack Gwynn. You'll hear Peter Grant. Listen . . .

Jack Gwynn: Good evening. This is Jack Gwynn. WLW-Radio, the Nation's Station, presents *Tribute To A Man Named Jim.*

Music:	"Jesus of Nazareth" Establish, fade, hold under for:
Jack Gwynn:	"When death comes, breaking into the circle of our friends, words fail us, our mental machinery ceases to operate, all our little stores of wit and wisdom, our maxims, our mottoes, accumulated from daily experience, evaporate and are of no avail. These things do not seem to touch or illuminate in any effective way the strange vast presence whose wings darken the world for us . . ."
Music:	Up for five seconds, fade, and hold under for:
Jack Gwynn:	Those words by the poet Edward Carpenter were written more than a hundred years ago. Yet, they seem so imminent. The broadcasting industry has lost a friend.

His name was James D. Shouse—Jim, to those who knew him well. Perhaps you as a listener didn't know him personally, but part of him was projected through every radio program you have heard during the past twenty-eight years. James D. Shouse was Chairman of the Board, Crosley Broadcasting Corporation. An impressive title— yes. But behind that title was a quiet man of simple tastes, a man who couldn't say no to a good idea no matter how difficult it would be to bring to reality.

James D. Shouse once said, "We must

[109]

be a considerate and constructive guest in America's homes or we will not be invited back." That was his philosophy when he joined the Crosley Broadcasting Corporation in 1937 as President. Twenty-four years later, James Shouse stood before an audience in New York and accepted the Broadcast Pioneer's First Annual "Mike Award" in behalf of WLW. It was for "dedicated service to its community, encouragement to radio artists and craftsmen, integrity and leadership." H. V. Kaltenborn made the presentation to Mr. Shouse that eventful night in 1961.

It was at that moment James Shouse knew he had accomplished what he set out to do: "to make WLW Radio and WLW Television considerate and constructive guests in America's homes." And perhaps, as Mr. Kaltenborn spoke, James Shouse's mind drifted back to 1937 . . . a big year in the golden era of radio . . .

Music: Theme to Moon River, scatterings of old programs and voices.

Jack Gwynn: Perhaps you remember those voices. Announcer Charles Woods. Organist Lee Erwin. Vocalists, the DeVore Sisters. The program: *Moon River*. It was apparent to James Shouse that the medium of radio presented a giant vehicle for entertainment —"down to earth" entertainment as well

[110]

	as the reporting of news and weather. So, it was in 1937 that he initiated his concepts of programming with effects that were to give the entire radio industry new goals to reach. In 1938, just one year after he arrived, thousands of midwesterners turned their radio dials to WLW and heard this:
Recording:	The seven beeps of the WLW time tone, then the theme into *Avalon Time* with Red Skelton.
Jack Gwynn:	That was the start of the actual broadcast in 1938 of *Avalon Time* with an up-and-coming comedian, Red Skelton, originating from the Nation's Station. Prior to Mr. Shouse's arrival, WLW-Radio was already known as the "Cradle of Stars." Mr. Shouse vowed he would fill that cradle to capacity—and it wasn't long before the parade began. The group you are about to hear came to Cincinnati from Belfontaine, Ohio, and soon thrilled listeners in a style that has remained unique for the past twenty-five years . . .
Music:	The Mills Brothers sing, fifteen seconds, then under for:
Jack Gwynn:	Yes, the Mills Brothers brought a special brand of happiness to millions of happy listeners. The WLW programming staff, under the leadership of Mr. Shouse, was always on the lookout for embryo talent. One day, in 1944, a young Cincinnati resi-

[111]

dent named Doris Kappelhoff walked into the studio. Nervous? Yes, but she was determined to show that she had what it took to reach the top. Here is how Doris Kappelhoff, now known as Doris Day, sounded on her original WLW audition twenty-one years ago . . .

Music: Doris Day recording, forty-five seconds, then under for:

Jack Gwynn: A year later, 1945, two rather shy sisters arrived from Maysville, Kentucky, to launch their careers. It wasn't long before WLW listeners were enjoying the blended voices of Rosemary and Betty Clooney. You are now going to hear the actual audition they made before a WLW microphone twenty years ago . . .

Music: Clooney Sisters, one minute, then under for:

Jack Gwynn: During the thirties and forties, radio announcers seemed to be just as famous as the stars. And WLW contributed its share of "men with the golden tongues." Don Hancock, John Cornell, Donald Dow, Floyd Mack, and Durwood Kirby, just to mention a few. But the one man who supplied the "backbone of comprehensive broadcasting" to WLW-Radio remained through the years contributing a special brand of precise, clear-cut reporting which many young announcers today would do

	well to emulate. Of course, I'm talking about Peter Grant who, with James Shouse, shared those early years of the golden age of radio. I'm quite sure he has many memories of his own. Right, Pete?
Peter Grant:	Indeed I have, Jack, and thank you for the kind words. You know, during these hectic days of space shots, world crises and the task of daily living, the "luxury" of reflection is often crowded out. We all like to recall those special moments in our lives which gave us particular pleasure. In my life, some of those moments certainly occurred during the golden age of radio—and I remember them well. I believe that one of Jim Shouse's primary aims was to "give the listener something to remember." In a way he carried on a tradition established by Powel Crosley in the early twenties. Of course, that's really going back, but do you realize that "Fats" Waller actually originated his program from WLW? And fortunately, the station has preserved many exciting moments from the past—and these include the one and only "Fats." Remember?
Tape:	Fats Waller. Fifteen seconds, then under for:
Peter Grant:	And if you recall "Fats" Waller, I'm sure you'll remember a gent who called himself "Singin' Sam, The Barbasol Man." Singin'

	Sam had a young assistant who also had a great deal of talent and, I might add, courage. The incomparable Jane Froman!
Tape:	Jane Froman, twenty-five seconds, then under for:
Peter Grant:	Yes, those were the golden years of radio, perhaps never to be equalled for their sheer ability to give the imagination wings. Remember the wit of Fred Allen? Remember the ingratiating Fanny Brice as Baby Snooks? Stoopnagle and Bud? Remember this familiar knock?
Tape:	Al Pearce, knocking, "Nobody's home, I hope-I-hope-I-hope"
Peter Grant:	And there were others like Orson Welles, who scared the daylights out of us. *The Aldrich Family, Kraft Music Hall, Rubinoff and His Magic Violin,* and a little fellow named Johnny, dressed in a red coat with brass buttons . . .
Tape:	Johnny's "Calllll for Philip Morris!"
Peter Grant:	And who, over forty, can forget those early soap operas? WLW practically pioneered the daytime serial, and radio's first soap operas originated here. It was called *The Life of Mary Sothern.* There were others: *The Mad Hatterfields . . . Midstream . . . The Puddle Family . . .* and best known of them all, *Ma Perkins* starring Virginia Payne.
Tape:	Ma Perkins, ten seconds, then under for:
Peter Grant:	I remember so well those early radio shows

[114]

like *Famous Jury Trials . . . Nation's Playhouse . . . Builders of Destiny* and especially one that Jack mentioned earlier: *Avalon Time.*

Tape: Avalon Time, 1:40 then under for:

Peter Grant: You know, at one point, WLW was originating a total of twenty-two shows per week which were fed to the networks! And during this period, the Cradle of the Stars continued to spawn some of the future greats in show business: Andy Williams, Dick Noel, Bill Nimmo, Ed Byron, The Ink Spots, Ramona, The Smoothies, Jeanette Davis, Tommy Riggs and his "alter ego" Betty Lou, Frank Lovejoy—and the list goes on and on. In the field of sports, WLW was fortunate to have such sportscasters as Red Barber and Al Helfer.

There's no doubt about it. Memories of WLW Radio in the thirties and forties will always remain most pleasant. But Jim Shouse didn't live in memories. He constantly made it a point to investigate and experiment. In 1942 a young lady named Ruth Lyons came to WLW and in a few short years became the Nation's Station's greatest star. Her first programs were *Morning Matinee* and *Petticoat Partyline.* Then she became hostess of a new program called *50-Club.* Do you remember how the *50-Club* sounded in 1949? Listen . . .

Tape: 50-Club, thirty seconds, then under for:

[115]

Peter Grant:	And the rest is history. I'm quite sure that if Jim Shouse had his way about it, he would frown on complicated eulogy, he would be embarrassed by praise, he would be hesitant in talking about his accomplishments. Therefore, I will respect that spirit of humility and end my portion of this evening's tribute by quoting a statement he made when he accepted the Golden Mike Award in behalf of WLW. "It has been an exciting adventure to be part of broadcasting almost since its beginning, and it is perhaps even more exciting to look forward to the future". . .
Music:	Sneak in behind Peter Grant, somber but spirited music.
Peter Grant:	Words spoken by a quiet but dynamic man, words unencumbered by rhetoric, unfettered by overstatement. This was *James* Shouse, Chairman of the Crosley Broadcasting Corporation. This was *Jim* Shouse, a man whom you could admire.
Music:	Up momentarily, then out.
Jack Gwynn:	Thank you, Pete. I agree, as does everyone at Crosley Broadcasting Corporation, that James Shouse would frown—and even become bored—with the praise he so richly deserves. He was a man who "moved," a man who never stopped in his desire to contribute every drop of energy he possessed to that which he loved best, "Giving people something to remember." In a

sense, he was an entertainer himself, not as a performer before a mike or camera, but rather as a "quiet influence" that hovered just outside the rim, gently prodding people into giving their best.

A perfect example of this took place in 1944, not in the field of entertainment, but in the field of war. At the time, Mr. Shouse was serving on a subcommittee of the U.S. Board of War Communications. He was suddenly called to Washington to attend a meeting. The committee asked his advice on building a series of 50-kilowatt short-wave stations to be used for broadcasting overseas. Mr. Shouse knew that Germany already had shortwave power in the neighborhood of 100 kilowatts, so he recommended that we use stations of 200 kilowatt power each! Not one manufacturer represented on the committee believed this to be technically feasible. Well, the meeting would have ended right then and there if James Shouse had agreed. Instead, he stepped out into a corridor, made a phone call to Chief Engineer Rockwell in Cincinnati, and asked if a series of 200-kilowatt transmitters could be built. Mr. Rockwell, with a moment's hesitation, said, "Yes"— and within ten minutes, Mr. Shouse convinced the committee that Crosley could build the new power shortwave facility. And, as you know, that facility was built in

Bethany, Ohio, an engineering feat unsur-
passed at that time for its daring and sheer
power.

To sum up the philosophy of James D.
Shouse, I guess you could say he was a man
who would never say "no." He was always
willing to listen and more than willing to
act upon his convictions. His four-point
program of engineering, programming,
talent, and community service will remain
as a goal for which we aim. We, who now
attempt to carry on James Shouse's ideals,
we who attempt to add to the framework
he built, would do well to keep in mind his
advice,

"We must be a considerate and constructive guest in America's homes. . . or we
will not be invited back."

Slight Pause
Jack Gwynn: . . . Thank you for taking these few mo-
ments to help remember a man named Jim.
Closing Music

The Shouse name continues, of course, via memories and
ideas of his still at work at the various stations. And, as it
must to all men of such position, via his name being on
an award given to college students in the area. The Avco
Broadcasting Corporation has this thing called the Shouse
Award, given each year to a handful of university seniors
whose bag in the academic treadmill has been broadcasting.
Says Avco, "What the students have in common is an
outstanding academic record at their various universities,

involvement in both classroom and extra curricular broad-cast projects, and a deep interest in making a contribution to the advancement of broadcasting as an industry. The winning students are selected by the faculty members of each university."

What exactly *is* the Shouse Award—given, they say, to perpetuate the pioneering spirit of imagination and inno-vation of Mr. Shouse during his Avco Broadcasting years? Well, each winner gets cash and each university gets cash and an inscribed bronze plaque for permanent display, and in addition to the cash, the students get hand-scrolled cer-tificates, suitable—as they say in the ads—for framing.

WLW throughout the years has done an awful lot of *innovating*, some of it being the sort they'd rather not have mentioned because a few were not exactly winners. I re-member back in 1938 when I was still in high school and thought Peter Grant was God, that I read one morning in the *Enquirer* that WLW was going to do more than make nice noises at it. Through some Rube Goldberg device, it was going to print a newspaper right there in my living room during the night while I slept. Then, when I awoke in the morning, there, in front of the radio—or wherever WLW planned to toss the thing—would be a newspaper almost like newspapers make. I was rather ex-cited about the idea. I think, at the time, WLW was, too.

The principle, of course, was based on radio-photos, the way newspapers send news pictures over the wires from one city room to another. In September, 1937, the FCC opened up a couple of broadcast frequencies so if anyone wanted to play that way, he could. One year later, Powel Crosley got the license to operate station W8XUJ for that purpose. The station had a thousand watts of power and operated on 26 megacycles, way down there on the broadcast band. Of course, I could never convince my parents to buy a facsimile receiver at the time so I never truly got involved with this wonderful idea, but no matter. For several years, after WLW signed off at 2 A.M., the facsimile transmitter was cranked on, and for an hour each night broadcast—or "printed"—news stories, news pictures, weather maps, police information, drawings, and even Bible verses. But they say no more than a hundred Cincinnatians had the facsimile receivers in their homes. In 1939 Crosley manufactured one, calling it *Reado*, which sold for $79.50, but my parents still refused to fork over the money, my father pointing out at the time that since we were on welfare, Roosevelt might take a dim view of such an expenditure.

Lichty describes the process which sloshed reading material out of your Atwater Kent. "During the one hour of transmission," he wrote, "about four or five feet of materials could be received on a six-inch wide continuous strip of paper. This chemically-treated paper turned from white to black (dark gray) when scanned by a spot of light; thus etching the image to be received."

Networks tried facsimile stuff, too. In 1938, at least, the Mutual Broadcasting System did. Its three member stations —WLW in Cincinnati, WGN in Chicago, and WOR in New York—hurled pictures at one another during the wee hours of the morning when their regular stations were napping. But the idea of facsimile broadcasting petered out; along came the war; along came television; and there you are. I suppose now I could get a tremendous deal on a facsimile receiver, but I have lost interest, too.

Now, ready or not, let's go visit the guy who runs the store today: John Murphy. Hand over your heart, lady! I sat once with him in his office and listened to him reminisce. Nice guy, really. A shrewd businessman, though, and I would hate to try to match wits with him in any corporation donnybrook. He knows whereof he speaks both in the world of talent, which broadcasting is, and in the world of business, which broadcasting also is. Also, he is from the Bronx which means little. Everybody has to be from somewhere. He started in the broadcasting business in the thirties as an NBC page boy when NBC pages were decked out even more stylishly than General MacArthur or General Patton ever dreamed possible. Also, he was a drummer in a neighborhood combo. Also, he remembers his first touch with radio: sitting in the Bronx with his mother listening to the 1924 Convention on a crystal set.

As a page—and as a musician—he lived in a golden world. He says he managed to work as an NBC page on Saturday afternoons when the network broadcast football games. He used to hang around the musicians who were on "standby" in case the game fell apart and the network was hard pressed for something to send along to its stations. "Benny Goodman," he recalled, "played saxophone as a house musician back then. The Dorsey brothers sat in, and so did Phil Napoleon." Who was on drums, fooling around? None other than Murphy himself. But he later swung over from page to the typing pool and soon gave up the drums. What forced his decision, he said, was a chance for his neighborhood band to play six nights a week at the Hunter Island Inn. He felt he couldn't do that and be in the typing pool at the same time, so he gave up music.

"The important thing," he says, "was did I want to grow with broadcasting or be a musician? Actually, I was making more money with my drums than I was at NBC, but my guardian angel was working overtime. Anyway, I knew in my heart I wasn't a *good* musician. I was a good musician, I suppose, because they said I had a beat. But I didn't really understand music. I was faking most of the time. So I took a hard look at broadcasting, where it was going, and how it was developing. About that time I had moved from the typing pool to the traffic department, the business side of broadcasting. The traffic department was where the stations along the network cleared for commercial programming. This was back in the mid-thirties. But the decision? Now that I look back on it, I have to admit I was getting guidance from Someone . . ."

WLW was one of the stations he called on after NBC put him on the road. When television came along, he wanted to get into it at station level. Dunville asked him to put WLWD in Dayton, Ohio, on the air—and the "greenies" have been flying ever since. Greenies? Well, Mr. Murphy sends out dozens—perhaps, thousands—of quickly scribbled notes each day, all in green ink, to whomever on the staff has need of such a note. Hence the name greenies. Paul Dixon recalls that one time he met Rosemary Kelly in the halls of WLWT, she waved a fistful of "greenies" at him, and said, "I'll trade you ten of mine for five of yours."

Murphy didn't stay long in Dayton. Dunville brought him down to WLWT, Cincinnati, in less than ten months to take over the management chores at the flagship station. Says Murphy, "Dixon was the big competition over at WCPO-TV, clobbering everybody. WLWT wanted me to do something about it."

Murphy is no Johnny-come-lately at working with programs and discovering talent. Wrote Paul Dixon once:

"Before he (Murphy) came to Cincinnati he had made several top discoveries. Who discovered Bob Smith—'Howdy Doody'—and brought him from Buffalo to New York and the big time? John Murphy, that's who. Who discovered Neal Van Ells in Terre Haute, Indiana, and brought him to WLWD to become one of the first big television announcers in the area? John Murphy, that's who. And who discovered electricity? Benjamin Franklin. Listen, John Murphy can't do it *all* himself!"

It was to John Murphy that Mel Martin resigned from the tube to go into the ministry. Says Murphy of this moment, "Some thought his interest in the ministry was phony, but I can tell anyone that's wrong. When Mel told me he wanted to leave for that reason—he was quite popular—I offered him a religious program on WLWT. He was polite but he said television would be completely contrary to his feelings. That's how he put it. I respected him for that. And I still respect him. Good people like Mel are wonderful to know—if only for a little while."

The man who heads up Avco Broadcasting loves live programming and even more, loves local live programming. "Besides," he points out, "it's good business to use local talent on WLW-Television. We can promote the Dixons and the Brauns and the Donahues and the Kellys. This gives us a sales advantage and a program advantage over our competition. We can build promotions around our people. It's a matter of finding the right talent, that's all. We've had our share of flops. Don't forget that. But our flops are few and far between."

Is he the typical establishment guy that the bearded street-people can't dig? No. If they knew what a free spirit he was, they'd groove with him completely. "Sure,"

[123]

he told Dixon once, "I go out on the limb all the time. Once you get into management, you have to—or you're doing nothing to earn your keep. And whatever you do, you have to be successful at it or you're in trouble. These are the facts of life I live with every day. The thing is, you can't be successful by standing still or doing nothing. I don't know which of us has the most fun, Paul. All I know is, when you're out there in front of that camera, you must make minute-by-minute and second-by-second decisions that concern *today*. Here I sit and make decisions that will affect Avco Broadcasting five, ten, fifteen years from now. It's fun—and it's rewarding, too. And it's no more frightening than watching someone putting one of those $20,-000 putts we see on televised tournaments. One difference is, the golfer sees the result right away. And there's another difference. Some of my decisions can cost the company a lot more than $20,000."

SAT in the control room the other day with Lou Barnett who twirls the knobs and fiddles with this and that, he being the audio engineer for the *Paul Dixon Show,* and suddenly I sensed that all of us—me, Lou, John Murphy, and the tower lights—were no longer spring chickens. It didn't seem like dozens of years had skitted by since W8XCT, the forerunner of WLWT, had sent out its first flickering flippity flopping picture back there in 1946 when there were only about a hundred receiving sets in the Cincinnati area. By 1947, W8XCT was cranking out twenty hours of television a week, people kept up with the Joneses by putting fake TV antennas on their roofs, and the rest of us—the poorer folk—attended whatever neighborhood bar had a television set. Those were, in retrospect, the "good old days" but as all "good old days" are, they didn't seem so at the time. Memories will ever be faulty and beautiful, won't they? No matter. The bars on Mc-

Millan Street, in the university area, got my business, I got their beer, and we all got to watch the test pattern.

In the late forties those of us attached to radio stations pretended not to be terribly excited about the new gadget that tossed moving pictures into the living rooms and bars of the Greater Cincinnati area. But the handwriting was on the wall, the seven-inch screen, and everywhere. Television was here to stay, streetcars weren't, and those were the facts of life. It would be pleasant, in this book about WLW, for me to say that WLW—or W8XCT—was the first television station that I, as a Cincinnati native, had ever gaped at, but, sorry, Mr. Murphy, it wasn't that way. The first time I saw television was in New York City. I was walking along a street, looked in a window, and there was a television set in the store window, laying pictures on me. I was not terribly impressed. I only stood there an hour, missing a luncheon engagement, making a girl terribly angry with me, and as the result, I returned to Cincinnati, stayed here, and met another girl. Broadcasting plays an important role in *all* our lives, doesn't it?

The first time I truly saw television in Cincinnati was in the company of James Crane, better known as Steve, who later became a vice president at Avco Broadcasting, but back then in our salad days we were toiling at WZIP, which was then in Covington and which was then owned by Arthur Eilermann. We had got free passes to watch the Reds play baseball, attended the game, but because the gentlemen hustling beer in the stands did not return to our location every five minutes, we left after two innings and sought out the nearest bar. There, in the shadow of Crosley Field, we twirled on bar stools, drank beer, and watched the rest of the game in comfort on the saloon's television. As Steve and I sat in the bar, watching the tube, we both agreed that television would never catch on as radio had.

To capsule the television era of Avco Broadcasting is simple chronologically. In 1949, WLWD went on the air in Dayton in that roller-rink-turned-television-palace. And WLWC went on the air the same year in Columbus, originating in a structure that served as studios, transmitter, and garage. In 1954, WLWT became NBC's first color affiliate, bringing us the New Year's *Tournament-of-Roses Parade*. The first *local* live color show was the *50/50 Club*, coming at us one hot day in August, 1957. The next day, there was the *Midwestern Hayride* decked out in color, too. It is also said that in 1959, WLWT colorcast the first daytime baseball game ever colorcast locally and regionally.

But dates do not tell the story of Avco Broadcasting's television years. People do—and what people were about! In the early days of television, Rod Serling was a member of the WLWT writing staff, doing whatever typing chores were required, doing his own in his spare time, the latter being notes and plays and playlets. He moved from WLW to WKRC where, in the company of a quickly-put-together stock company, he put on a series of local dramas called *The Storm*, the scripts for which he tucked away for hitting the big-time, selling them for production to the live hour drama shows the networks then offered us in profusion. One of his first scripts was a powerful play called *Patterns*, the study of corporate life. Some say he based it on the corporate life that existed at WLW, but others say he didn't, and anyway, what does it matter in the final analysis? He has become one of America's better writers (I see his picture all the time touting the Famous Writers' correspondence course and I hear him peddling pharmaceuticals via television commercials) and Avco Broadcasting has become one of America's better broadcasting devices, so let us move on.

In the early days of "live" television—which WLW stations *still* produce like (or as) Mother used to make—there was a degree of casual electricity pervading the halls of the stations. If a mistake was made, there it was for the world to see. Now, with the advent of videotape, most commercials are taped and retaped until they are just what the doctor—meaning the sponsor—wants. But in those days I used to pop into WLW every couple of days as an advertising agency producer, my chore being to supervise the "live" commercials for our agency client, the Kroger Company. Know going in that an agency producer in a television station is a guest. WLW had—and has—its own competent staff of production people. These are the ones who make most advertising agency producers look better than the advertising agency producers really are. At least, in the WLW stations they do. But perhaps my experiences with live commercials can show the awfulness of live television, at least from a sponsor's point of view.

The Kroger Company, during these early days of television, had been rightfully impressed with the food commercials that ran weekly on the network production of the *Kraft Playhouse*, an hour-long live drama. The commercials showed food being prepared—all live—and the commercials were good. The fact that the network had a cast of thousands (well, almost) to do these commercials meant little. The agency and the sponsor decided that anything New York did on the tube, Cincinnati and WLW could duplicate, so the matter was dumped in my lap.

Timing in cooking is of the essence—and to have the

souffle rise on cue, to fit in with the commercial break on *Meet Corliss Archer*, takes timing, skill, a few prayers, and, upon occasion, a few curses. Cooking was ever thus. The WLW director, and I, the agency producer, used to sit in the control room each week with our fingers crossed, hoping the water would boil at the right minute, the eggs would fry, the toaster would pop up on cue, and that nothing untoward happened during the airing of the commercial. On another station in Cincinnati there used to be a cooking show where the (then) galloping gourmet would occasionally find her earrings dropping into the salad or the mashed potatoes. Jean Cunningham, dietician and charming gal, used to tell us every week not to worry, even though we gave her such impossible assignments as making a complete salad (with Kroger produce, of course) in one minute, from hacking up the stuff to serving it, garnished, in salad bowls. Each week we gave her impossible tasks; each week she saved us; and after each show, I went to the nearest bar and had a few. WLW had worked another miracle.

There were, on the other hand in those early days of television, miracles which WLW couldn't work. Once a man took it upon himself to perch on the rim of the Carew Tower, one of our tallest buildings, and lead those watching below to believe he was about to do himself in. WLW, being downtown with its studios, merely set up a camera on the street outside its door, tilted the camera upward, got a closeup shot with a long lens, and put the picture on the air. Meanwhile, up at WCPO-TV where I was working as a director, we were reasonably disturbed because we were far up on a hill, looking down on Cincinnati, and though we rolled a camera outside, got a picture with the longest lens we had, all we could show was the Carew Tower and that was it. The man had positioned himself so that he was around the corner, we couldn't get a picture of him, WLW could—and listen, that can hurt a fellow's pride. I called WLW, got the director who shall be nameless (we had once both been fired from the same station, an act that made us blood brothers), and told him my plight.

"Okay, Dick," my friend said. "We're sending a newsman up there on the building where he is. I'll see if we can't talk the guy into moving around the corner and sitting on the other ledge so you can get a picture of him, too."

And he gave it the old school try, but instead of moving around so we could get a picture of him, the man on the ledge got discouraged, I suppose, and came back inside— and that was that. Tragic story, really, and I don't mean to make fun of one man's suffering, but the point is television directors operate with a detachment that at times makes even the hardest criminal worry. But all television directors—and all broadcast personnel—belong to a club of sorts. WLWT and WCPO-TV were, and still are, as competitive as you'd ever find, but a bond exists between the peons who toil in the hire of both. Television used to be like that. That was when everybody got fired a lot. Now television has settled down a little.

Lee Hornback, by the way, has been my friend for a number of years. He used to direct the *Paul Dixon Show* when it originated from WCPO-TV, but he got fired. Now he's doing corporate things for WLW, *all* of WLW —which means Avco television. Some of the engineers, like Roy Smith, who used to run camera when I was directing at WCPO-TV, are now in the hire of WLW.

Abe Cowan, formerly program director of WLWT, used to run camera and later direct at WCPO-TV before coming to Crosley Square—and now he's somewhere else. Through the years WLW has managed to accumulate and hold on to most of the real professionals of local television, those in front of the camera as well as those behind it.

But things have settled down, or seem so to me. No one at Avco Broadcasting seems to get terribly excited about the sky falling down these days. Most are professionals for whom the sky has fallen so much the event is about as upsetting as a sneeze. The crews behind the scenes— cameramen, audio men, floor men, lighting men, prop boys, transmitter engineers, and even the roving shoeshine man—seem unflappable. Now and then a documentary will come along that unflaps them, financially and otherwise, but I have the feeling that everyone there, missing the excitement of the good old days, looks forward to these moments.

The documentaries, like Gene McPherson's beautiful and heartbreaking *The Last Prom*, originate with a variety of people. An Avco Broadcasting documentary might cost up to $50,000 to make. Consider, for instance, *The Last Prom*, a filmed documentary on driving accidents during nights of high school prom exuberance. Said Gene Mc- Pherson, "*The Last Prom* keeps being repeated. It was made originally in 1963 in black-and-white. So we re- made it again, all in color—and that costs money. But it does a good community service job which is the important thing. Prints of it have been shown around the world as well as all over the United States. Schools have shown it in auditoriums. Safety groups everywhere have shown it. We sell prints of it to other stations. The important thing is, the message gets across." Among the other award-winning documentaries are Don Dunkel's *All the Fun Is Getting There*, a study of old people, and Tom Robertson's *Appalachian Heritage*.

One WLWT director, when involved in all phases of public service, recalled the time he produced the Easter Mass—for television origination, that is—from first this church and that church. "The problem," he said, "is the long processional. One time somebody at St. Peter's got the cues mixed up, cued the processional before it was to start, we weren't even on the air yet, and there went the processional, horns tooting, everything. I wasn't the director on that one, but I remember the director screaming into the intercom that connected him with the production men inside the church, 'Hold the processional! Hold the processional!' Somehow it was managed, but it wasn't easy . . ."

Another time:

"I remember once," said another director, "doing a remote from a church in Westwood. It was in color. All of a sudden, the minister stops on me, dead. I look at the clock I had in the remote truck and I see we have four minutes left over to fill. There we were on a network feed! But the minister was right and we were wrong. The clock in the remote truck didn't keep time too well (none of us knew this) but the minister was going by *his* watch, which was accurate. He had got us off in time but we didn't know it!"

Such television directors, by dint of the many religious telecasts they have put together for Avco Broadcasting, could easily give religious instruction to prop men, but they are much too busy now, involved in other projects. Communions in the Catholic Mass were always one director's nightmare—technically, that is. "When we do a Mass," he said, "we try to do all the Mass, but how do you get them to speed it up when time is running out so you can get the Communion in? All you can do is sit in the remote truck, watch the time disappear, and pray right along with them. To be honest, now and then a priest, aware the people at home have need of the service as a complete unit, too, will skip over a couple of prayers if we can get a cue to him. This isn't as awful as it might sound when you consider the number of people who can't get to church— old people in old folks homes and the rest. Through Avco Broadcasting and the generosity of the churches, we can bring the services to them. This is most important and, once again, we don't make a dime on it. We lose money every time, but we feel we owe this to the community."

Not *all* the technical problems are of a religious nature. Consider the Cincinnati Zoo series which was telecast live at first and then, upon occasion, taped. Recalled still another director, "It was fun, I suppose. Zoo personnel kept bringing animals to the studio. Once they even brought this elephant. Well, with the way our building is arranged, all props—even elephants—have to be taken to the studios upstairs by elevator. The elephant wasn't too happy about the prospect—and how do you explain to an elephant that an elevator ride is fun? And suppose Mr. Murphy had come walking through the place at that moment with a client? I mean, what do you say when the elevator door opens and he and the client look in and see me standing there with this dumb elephant? Suppose the client is a Democrat?"

Or, take the matter of sea turtles which the studio crew

wished some other station had done. One prop boy told me, "The doggone thing wasn't housebroken and the show was live and—well, it was a sight to behold. Outside the studio, waiting to come in and tape their show, was a bunch from the University of Cincinnati but the setup man from that show wouldn't come in until we had cleaned up the sea turtle mess. That wasn't a happy day for floor men. I went home, my wife asked me what was new, and I almost hit her . . ."

Animals of every description have honored the studios —and upon occasion the floors—of Avco Broadcasting. Bob Braun has tinkered with the idea of wrestling a bear that one entrepreneur brought by. Paul Dixon, wise man, decided he wanted nothing whatsoever to do with the beast. Monkeys have got loose in the accounting department at the square. They had a field day, throwing papers all over the place. Birds get loose in the studio. One was loose for three weeks in the studio where Ruth Lyons held forth on the 50/50 Club. It used to swoop down and shatter the ids of the ladies in attendance, then retreat back up to the ceiling in that darkened tangle of wires and lights and gloom, where it would perch, peer down with disenchantment, then swoop about again. When snakes and alligators come to the studios, the engineers running camera break out the longest lenses they have. When the snakes start crawling, the cameramen start backing, and when they reach the door, exit—fast. Once a raccoon got loose in the elevator shaft, hiding and cavorting up and down the elevator cables. One director still keeps a snake-bite kit in his office.

"You never know," he said.

So, I suppose, television really hasn't settled down *that* much after all.

There was the program called *Signal Three*, a safety show aimed at children; winner of nineteen awards, including the Peabody Award. But awards are old hat to Avco Broadcasting. There's the Alfred Sloan Safety Award. *Signal Three* won that for the station and, much to his pleasure, the sponsor. There's the Freedom Foundation Award. The Christians and Jews Brotherhood Award. Actually, Avco Broadcasting has accumulated enough placques to deplete a good-sized forest. Public service was and is and will forever be rather rampant among the stations of Avco Broadcasting. Consider the program that used to run, Peter Grant and the FBI's (then) Ed Mason, a five minute thing called *You and The Law*. Avco Broadcasting, via a college conference show, drew upon the resources and students of sixty-three different colleges and universities in the area. "The problem," groaned a producer of the university telecast, "was topics. After running through about 230 topics, listen, you can run dry. Still, the show won the Peabody Award."

Another public service thing was the helicopter that hovered over Cincinnati as Art Mehring, strapped in and peering down, gave Cincinnatians traffic information and whatever struck his fancy. He was a Cincinnati policeman who, when he retired, joined Avco Broadcasting full time, still doing 'copter reports until he passed away. Wonderful guy, that Art Mehring. Though WLW claims, at times, to have started him in broadcasting, he actually first went on television back in 1951 on WCPO-TV on a program called *Police Blotter*, a five-minute dab that ran during the dinner hour Monday through Friday. I am sure of this because I wrote, produced and directed the program. I was also the floorman and typist. And had I known how to change towels in the towel rack in the men's room I might

[135]

have had that job, too, but as you can see I lacked the versatility needed to become a professional television guy. Each afternoon Art Mehring would toot up to WCPO-TV in his police car and read, over the air, the script I had written on what we used as a substitute for a TelePrompTer: our own typewriter that typed in great big type, letters an inch high. As the script, on a long roll, unrolled, Art read the thing—and that, pretty much, was our act. Few things upset Art because he was a fine gentleman. One day, though, typing the script on the huge roll moments before air time, I ran into a problem. The *E* fell off the typewriter. Have you ever tried to write anything—even a threatening note—without using an *E?* So I left the script half done, put it on the roll down, and rather than worry Art, told him nothing about it. The camera came on, he started reading, and—well, suddenly, mid-sentence, his script ended and there he sat with a minute to go. He grinned at me, off camera, and plunged ahead, doing far better by himself. After that, he did the program without script. He got to be himself—and that was good enough for Cincinnati. Glenn Ryle, now Skipper Ryle at WKRC-TV, was the announcer on *Police Blotter*, peddling the merits of the (then) *Cincinnati Post* which Art and I used to set fire to while Glenn held it up to the camera. Television, in those days, was rather freewheeling, I guess. But we didn't burn down any of the studios, if that helps.

Avco Broadcasting has gone into the business of 'copter traffic reports. Captain Dan alerts the motorists in that city of perfect traffic jams, Washington, D.C., where Avco Broadcasting operates WWDC and WWDC-FM. Lieutenant Jim Stanley of the Cincinnati Police Department is presently WLWT's traffic 'copter cop, and is carrying on

[136]

in the fine—and gabby—tradition of the late Art Mehring.

WLWC in Columbus went on the air April 3, 1949, on channel three instead of channel four where it is now, with such items as Sally Flowers (and her hats), Spook Beckman, and, later, Dean Miller, Nick Clooney, Jack Davis, and Jack Denton. News director Hugh DeMoss is an award-winning local, his news programs winning area Emmy Awards and he himself the only recipient of the area's only Television Academy Award for Individual Performance. Since 1949, its first year, WLWC has telecast the Ohio State University football games and in 1951 was the first station to present live television coverage of the Ohio High School AA Basketball State Finals from the Fairground Coliseum. This isn't bad when you consider that when WLWC first went on the air there were only eighty-eight receivers out there in televisionland. But within weeks the number of sets was up into the hundreds—and there, Sally Flowers, you are! What did the eighty-eight receivers (and who knows how many viewers each) watch those first weeks? Well, they watched the *Olympus Minstrels*, *Travel Time*, *Baldwin by Request*, and test patterns. The first day WLWC was on the air two and a half hours, took a dinner break, then came back for three more hours in the evening. A viewer, though, wrote in from Murdock, Minnesota, 720 miles away, to say that WLWC was coming in fine! By the end of WLWC's first year, the station was cranking out eighty-five hours of television per week, but Murdock, Minnesota, was never heard from again.

Said WLWC in a *Columbus Dispatch* ad, 1969, to its friends:

"A muddy cornfield with its small concrete-block build-

[137]

ing and tall steel tower was about to emanate something excitingly new. Central Ohioans were crowded around a few TV sets in anticipatory delight. Then, at precisely 3:00 P.M., April 3, 1949, there was the WLWC test pattern . . . The early days had their fun-to-remember moments. A field mouse caused havoc during an interview with a female guest. After setting up for the first remote telecast, the Red Bird game was rained out . . ."

Over there in Indianapolis, another Avco television station is part of the local scene: WLWI, Channel 13. From it, coverage of that Memorial Day Classic that has everyone in Indianapolis bananas: the 500-mile race. And over there in Dayton, WLWD, where the *Phil Donahue Show* originates. And out there in San Francisco sits KYA radio, swinging with the young transistor crowd. And on and on . . .

But, for our purposes, let us sing whatever love songs we have left at WLW—the four stations around here that send pictures at us, the radio station that Crosley started, and the people contained therein. Elmer William Hinkle no longer tells of hog prices from the Cincinnati stockyard—and no longer do Hink and Dink amuse us. Rosemary Kelly, on the other hand, a local television fixture went away for awhile but Avco Broadcasting brought her Irish warmth back to all of us again. Vivienne Della Chiesa came—and went. WLWT has come a long way since it included the television debut of *Boston Blackie* and carried one of the first paid political telecasts with Alben Barkley in 1948. Much time has passed since "live wrestling" originated at Mount Olympus where now educational station WCET would have us wrestle with our minds. Remember the first network feeds—*Cincinnati at Sunset* and

[138]

Dude Ranch Holiday? Remember the Pontifical Requiem Mass for Archbishop John T. Nicholas, the services in connection with the installation of the new archbishop, all of it, oh, all of it? Remember when WLWT brought Jerry Lester to town as part of a three-day Television Jubilee at Music Hall? He inaugurated WLWT's new $100,000 studios at Crosley Square in 1951—and also got Ruth Lyons mad at him which got all the women in Cincinnati mad at him, but listen, no one is perfect. Remember when the *Midwestern Hayride* and *Strawhat Matinee* (which first brought us wonderful Marian Spelman) originated from here as summer replacement for Sid Caesar and Imogene Coca on the *Show of Shows?* Remember Kate Smith?

Okay, so here I sit reminiscing. Fifty years ago, as of 1972, this gadget called WLW began. There is, really, too much to remember. There are those of you, I'm sure, who upon reading these pages will say, "He left out _____" and you will fill in a name that has meaning to you. There are those of you who will say, "He should have told about when _____ happened" and you will fill in that sweet memory of your own. I am aware of this and I am sure of the futility of trying to put between the pages of any book the half century of people and things and events that can properly be called this thing: WLW. Some things I have glossed over. Some things I have looked at (harder and deeper and with more fondness than the subject might have required) should have been glossed over. But don't you see? This is my WLW. There are as many WLW's as there are people.

The recent years of WLW—and all the people those years contain— are still fresh in our memory. Indeed, the people are still there, for the most part, talking at us. Tom Atkins is a guy I meet every night on the tube. I see Tony Sands a lot. Richard King doesn't come into my home any more and I regret this. Gene Randall got married—and thousands upon thousands of female watchers regret *that*. Frank Pierce, happily, is still among those present. Ruby Wright—bless her!—still pops up on the tube now and then to cheer me. Colleen Sharp is there. So is Bonnie Lou. So is . . . but the list is too long.

This business of broadcasting—television and radio— is at the same time a satisfying and fleeting business. Much great community good can be done as Avco Broadcasting can attest. But to broadcast—with sound only or with pictures that move and talk—is to write great and silly messages on the wind. These messages are hurled into the sky from great towers and some of them are caught, momentarily, in gadgets called radio and television receivers. But in an instant they are gone forever, never to return. To write for broadcasting is to write on wind. The new breeze comes along to blow away the sonnet and the silliness. As a kid I used to think that somewhere up in the sky, tooting around lonesomely, were radio signals from yesteryear, signals that did not dissipate, but went on and on—and only my lack of a special receiver kept me from pulling antique broadcasts out of the sky and back to me again. But they are gone, aren't they? Norman Brokenshire will never say again to me "How do you do, how do you do?" Ruth Lyons will never sing in her wild, sweet manner, "Let me entertain you." Art Mehring will never tell me of traffic tie ups, Howard Chamberlain will never moderate "World Front," and on and on and on. Never ever again.

[140]

One summer I attended the Ohio State Fair which, through the efforts of Avco Broadcasting as well as many others, has become a humdinger of a fair. I stood in the warm sun of morning and noon on the dirt track where later sulkies would race. I looked up into the grandstands —a solid mass of humanity—as they all concentrated on the makeshift stage upon which first Paul Dixon and later Bob Braun performed. But for some strange reason, I could not see any of their faces; there were too many. Yet, they saw Dixon. They saw Braun. This, too, is broadcasting in some way. I looked over to where Johnny Murphy stood, by the side of the stage, out of the spotlight, and I sensed somehow everything was one: the stands full of humanity, Dixon, Braun, Murphy, the television cameras, the blue sky, the noise, the beauty of all of it. And for one brief moment I knew, really knew, what broadcasting was all about.

It is people.

Only that and nothing more.

So let us look at WLW-Television as it was and is—only yesterday and now. Television is people. Perhaps, what WLW stands for can best be expressed by a closeup of four people: Bob Braun, Phil Donahue, Paul Dixon, and Ruth Lyons. They are diverse but they have one thing in common: each in his own way loved and still loves the viewer and the listener. A look at them, closely, will give us a better picture of where television has been and where it's going than all the projected statistics I could make up —and that's what I usually do with statistics anyway.

Let us look at Bob Braun, then Phil Donahue, then Paul Dixon, but leading the parade was WLW herself: Mrs. Herman Newman.

In 1942 Mrs. Herman Newman—Ruth Lyons—joined the staff of WLW. In 1967—a quarter of a century later—she retired. In between a lot happened. Trouble is, to write of Ruth Lyons is no simple task. She has been both deified and damned, more of the former than the latter; she has touched so many lives their names would fill the Manhattan telephone book; she changed the face of television, indeed—around here—she *made* the face of television; she has done this, said that, and—oh, all of it! What I mean is, where do I begin?

Sat once in the dining room of the Algonquin Hotel in New York talking with the editor-in-chief of a major publishing house (now forever nameless) plus the usual assortment of business-types that travel with same (sales managers, literary agents, promotion men, and always some bosomy chick in a mini skirt whose endowments were more obvious than the reason for her presence), and, to make a long story short, they were all enthused about a book they wanted me to write.

"It will sell," said the editor, "thousands and thousands more copies than all your other books put together."

"Wow," I said.

"It will make you rich," said the literary agent.

"Wow," I said.

"It will sell in drug stores, book stores, grocery stores, gasoline stations, pizza parlors, war surplus stores, beauty parlors, donut shops, and everywhere," murmured the sales manager of the publishing house.

"Wow," I said.

"You will be famous beyond your wildest expectations," whinnied the child in the mini skirt and the other endowments herewith noted. "You could wear tennis sneakers to dinner at the Four Seasons Restaurant."

"Wow," I said.

There was a long pause because they all sat looking at me.

"Well?" said the editor.

"I'll give it the old school try," I said. "But on the other hand, don't expect too much. I've never written the New Testament before."

"We are not talking about a religious book," the sales manager said. "We are talking about a book about a person."

"Ruth Lyons," said the editor.

"And like that," said the girl in the mini skirt, a charmer, but vaguely not with it.

"It," said the editor, "will be an unauthorized edition. That is, you'll write it without her approval. That way you can tell *all*."

[144]

"All what?" I said.

"All," said the editor.

"And like that," said the chick.

This was before Ruth Lyons had decided to write her delightful *Remember With Me.* Paul Dixon's *Paul Baby,* via World Publishing, had proved such a winner that major publishers had looked over the rest of the WLW-Television lineup to see if they, too, could come up with a winner. They had already approached Ruth Lyons, but she—busy with other things—had little time to consider the project. So they plied me with booze, bonbons, and visions of sugarplum fairies, figuring I was their boy. To write a book about anyone, unauthorized, is legal and aboveboard. It means, simply, that the subject of the book doesn't look over the script and mutter, "Gee, I wish you had written me better. There are a few discrepancies: my eyes are blue, not green; I did not invent the cotton gin; and I could not very well have three wives as you suggest because the first one is still married to me." The *reason* people like unauthorized versions of biographies, I suppose, is the writer is free. If the subject of the book has warts, the writer can say so. If the subject isn't as nice as his press agent would have the world believe, the writer can say so. Thus the reader, usually a grubby sort himself with more warts than anyone would desire, is privy to a side of the public figure the public doesn't usually see.

"There must be a lot of people out there—" the editor waved his hand to indicate west of the Hudson River where us squares live "—who hate her guts. Get quotes from them."

"We'll really sell," said the sales manager.

"And you'll be rich," said the agent.

[145]

"And like that," said the cutie.

"Thanks," I said, "but no thanks. Get somebody else."

"But why?"

"There are some things I won't do for money," I said. "And put down Ruth Lyons is one of them."

And there you are. Point is, I'm not an exposé kind of writer and anyway, Ruth Lyons had been before the public so much and given of herself so honestly, there's really nothing to expose which, even if there was, I wouldn't do anyway. I mean, why? People whose lives—and in her case, her very soul—are splashed each day on the tube should be allowed to go home, close the door, kick their shoes off and relax. I would no more intrude in that area of a performer's life than I would get other people to say awful things about them.

The question is, how do I tell of Ruth Lyons here? I have never personally *met* the lady. I have never even talked to her on the telephone. I got a letter from her once, but I don't think she really sent it. It was a promotion thing addressed to "occupant." But, over the years, I have been aware of her and her effect on the Midwest that we both love. Every time I drive up Colerain Avenue, through the Mt. Airy section where Bob Braun now lives, I can't help but remember the time she announced on the *50/50 Club* that she was going out after the show to buy Halloween candy for the kids who might be calling that evening. By eight that night police had to be called in. Traffic on Colerain was bumper-to-bumper, in each car a costumed child and mother, calling on Ruth Lyons. Said Ruth Lyons the next day on her show, "A few of the old girls came out to see me last night. . . ."

Let me tell about Ruth Lyons *this* way. While gathering

[146]

information for this book I spent a delightful afternoon with two of my favorite people: Mary Wood of the Cincinnati *Post & Times-Star* and Elsa Sule who has been with the 50/50 *Club* since the Civil War. Mary Wood, nursing her white bloody mary, had worked at and was fired from WLW the year after Ruth Lyons came over from WKRC. Elsa Sule, nursing a cold, had been at WLW since she graduated from the University of Cincinnati where she majored in peanut butter. Sit in with us and reminisce.

Mary Wood, recalling the early days, said, "When I first met Ruth, Elsa wasn't there. Elsa came later. Ruth came over from WKRC. The reason she came to WLW was that WLW was shopping around for good talent; she had been a real success over at WKRC; WLW wanted a noon show for the ladies on WSAI which it then owned; so Ruth was called. But Ruth was terribly loyal to the Tafts who operated WKRC. When she was told WLW would give her ten or twenty dollars more, I forget which, than she was getting at WKRC, she said she couldn't accept until she talked it over with Hub Taft, one of the truly nice men in broadcasting around here. She told Hub Taft that she really wanted to stay at WKRC, but as far as a raise went, WKRC said there was no way they could give it to her. So for no more than twenty dollars, WLW got the most valuable property the station has even known. . ."

Her days at WKRC had been wonderful, unpredictable, and at times wild. The wonder of radio had impressed Ruth Lyons while she was still in high school. She wrote once that, "I was in constant demand as an accompanist and pianist at local stations. And I was completely fascinated by this new enigma. I would rush home after a fifteen-minute session in one of the first velvet-draped isolation booths

[147]

ever built to find my mother frantically and vainly still trying to tune me in with a cat-whisker tracking over a strange little crystal gadget." After a spell at the University of Cincinnati she hired out at WKRC for $25 a week where just about everything happened. Ruth Lyons recalled that, "There was one night a well-known basso profundo guest singer, and among his selections was the booming *Song of the Volga Boatmen*. Just as he launched into the lusty boatman's favorite mood music for 'totin that barge' down the Volga, the studio door opened and in came four of the station personnel, wrapped in overcoats, their heads bound with turbans from towels from the men's room, dragging by heavy ropes, in perfect rhythm to the purple-faced boatman's chant, a full-sized gray coffin in which sat another staff pixy clutching a bunch of beets and clad in a raccoon coat, circa 1930! The basso received the accolade of all concerned—he never missed a beat of that measured dirge of the Muscovites—but he nearly popped a number of blood vessels later in one of the most beautiful tantrums of outraged dignity that it has ever been my pleasure to witness."

WKRC's loss was WLW's gain!

Said Mary Wood, "At WLW, Ruth started a show called *Petticoat Partyline*. Actually it was broadcast over WSAI, owned at that time by Crosley. It was a noontime luncheon show. Then came the show called *Morning Matinee* which she did for years. It led into what is now the *50/50 Club*. It used to originate from the Hotel Gibson. Paul Jones was her announcer. I'll never forget the first show there. It was in one of those dining rooms, women were invited, games like musical chairs were played, and prizes would be given away: hats. I went to see the show

[148]

and went back to the *Post*, where I was working, and blasted it to pieces. I said it was a silly show. I said all they did was play musical chairs and wear funny hats. Only then, I started *listening* to it, really listening to it. I knew Ruth was going to be a tremendous talent because she is so outspoken."

"Did Ruth Lyons appreciate your review of her early show?" I said.

"She was furious," Mary Wood said, grinning. "I told her I had written what I felt was the truth. She answered, 'Well, so the first show wasn't good. Give it a chance.' I did and it blossomed. When television came along, Ruth was ready for it. Almost."

"Almost?"

According to Mary Wood, Ruth Lyons answers that question herself. Simply put, Ruth Lyons in those radio days was fat. "I mean she was five by five," said Mary Wood. But Ruth Lyons took one look at herself on those kinescopes of the show—and she went on a diet. "I hadn't seen her for awhile," said Mary Wood, "so when I ran into her a month later at WLW I almost fainted. She had lost fifty or sixty pounds—and she has never gained it back. She started out by drinking nothing but fruit juice for three days. Then, she went on a diet and the weight just peeled off."

"Everybody and his brother," I complained, "is going to be asking what her diet was."

"Well," said Mary Wood, "I guess it was just that she cut down on food. It was fruit juice and coffee at first, I think. Besides, she was determined to lose weight. When Ruth is determined to do something, she *does* it."

James Maxwell, one of Cincinnati's finest writers, once

[149]

did a word picture of Ruth Lyons for the *Saturday Evening Post*. In the April 6, 1957, edition, he wrote that "with an incredible mixture of acid and treacly sentimentality she rattles on with a complete lack of self-consciousness about her enthusiasms and prejudices, her husband, child and maid, her preferences in food and her taste in music, the family lives of her associates on the program, articles and books she has read, politics, religion and almost anything else that pops into her mind. Alternately she browbeats, praises, ridicules and jokes with her staff and studio audience. All of this is done with expert showmanship, but without either script or format."

Radio was good for her, but television was better. I had listened to Ruth Lyons on radio and, to me, she came across okay but she seemed not exactly the sensation that she was until television came around. She was made for television—and television seemed made for her. Said Mary Wood, "Ruth told me once that whenever she had something to say, she said it. This was one of her greatest charms. One time I had written a column that displeased a few readers, I told Ruth about it, and she said, 'Mary, don't worry about it. I'll tell you something about this business. The longer you're in it, two things happen. The people who don't like you will either get used to you or die. The ones who complain most about the *50/50 Club* are the ones who never miss it—and it probably works the same for your column, too.'"

"Was there ever a time," I asked, "that Ruth Lyons battled for a principle or ideal and lost?"

Elsa Sule, sitting quietly, perked up. "I never saw her lose one, did you, Mary?"

[150]

"Nobody's right all the time," said Mary Wood, "and Ruth Lyons knew this, even of herself."

"Yes," said Elsa Sule, "but I never saw her lose a battle. If there was a commercial on the show she felt wasn't good, or a product, she wouldn't do it or take it."

"Actually," said Mary Wood, "I think Ruth Lyons was before her time, don't you? In some of the ways she thought."

"There were many times that Miss Lyons and I didn't agree," said Elsa Sule, "but with us, it was always a matter of opinion. She is violently and vehemently against the war in Vietnam—and she will tell you why in great detail at the drop of the hat."

"If Ruth Lyons were on the air today?" I said.

Elsa Sule grinned. "If Miss Lyons were on the air today, the war in Vietnam would be over."

"And what would she have said about today's youth?" I said.

Elsa Sule, who talks daily with Ruth Lyons by telephone, didn't hesitate: "Well, she liked the college kids and she would have said on the air that the majority of them are good. As for the minority, she would have said they may have a point, fighting for whatever they're fighting for. But she would have gotten mad if somebody tossed a bomb into a building."

Yes, the *50/50 Club* with Ruth Lyons was real, terribly real. James Maxwell wrote that once on the air, after light banter, "suddenly Ruth's mood changed completely. 'I was feeling fine when I got up this morning,' she announced somberly, 'but now I feel terrible.' She then recounted a story of Russian troops firing upon Hungarian women who

[151]

wanted to place wreaths upon the grave of the Unknown Soldier. 'What kind of a world are we living in when that can happen after so many years of so-called civilization?' she said. The audience made clucking noises of dismay. Ruth glowered at them. 'But you and I have no right to be smug,' she said angrily. 'On the same newscast I heard about a minister being beaten up by a mob in Tennessee because he was taking six Negro children to a newly-integrated high school.' She then launched into a lengthy and bitter denunciation of segregation and race prejudice. . . Ruth dropped the subject of race relations as abruptly as she had taken it up. 'I wanted to blow my stack and I did it,' she said. 'Now I feel better.' The remainder of the program was mostly small talk between Ruth, Willie Thall, Ruby Wright and Cliff Lash, with participation by the audience encouraged."

"What," I asked Elsa Sule, "made Ruth Lyons happy?"

"Candy," said Elsa. Candy was Ruth's daughter. "And Miss Lyons loved show business people. If she got someone good on the show, that made her happy. If she got into a good discussion or a good fight on the show, that made her happy. I remember once when she asked if Italian movie stars all really had dirt under their fingernails. The guest got upset but when the discussion was over, they both agreed that Italian movie stars were dirty."

Once, too, Ruth Lyons tangled with Gloria Swanson. Since Ruth Lyons had a running gag about her own advanced age, the first thing she said when Gloria Swanson came on camera was:

"Well, at last I have somebody on this show who is older than I am."

Later, when discussing one of Gloria Swanson's earlier

movies, Ruth Lyons—still playing with the running gag—said:

"Why *I* remember that. I must have been in kindergarten at the time."

Gloria Swanson chilled and said. 'Teaching, no doubt."

"We practically had to defrost the studio after *that* program," Elsa Sule recalled.

Yes, that was—and *is*—Ruth Lyons.

She was a person of likes and dislikes. *Strong* ones. Said Mary Wood of Mrs. Newman, "Arthur Godfrey came *after* Ruth Lyons. She was on television long before he was. Godfrey was on radio, then, but not television. Ruth was one of the original pioneers of daytime television shows of this sort."

Elsa Sule agreed, adding that "Miss Lyons' show was a radio retread in a way, though. She just moved it from radio to television. She added a few visual features but basically it was a radio show. I was originally hired to write scripts for *Morning Matinee* on radio which was just fine with me because the show was completely ad libbed. But the station had to have scripts in a file. Miss Lyons would grade them every day and that was as far as they went: from me to Miss Lyons to the filing cabinet. Nobody ever read anything from them on the air."

"Every now and then," said Mary Wood, "the station would give Ruth a promotion announcement to read. She'd try it but it never sounded like her. Besides she didn't want to *read*. She wanted to *talk*. To be honest, she never could read a script."

"She sounds a little like the female version of *The Man Who Came to Dinner*," I said.

"Or *luncheon*," Elsa grinned. Then she got serious. "It

makes me real mad. Miss Lyons has been a good friend but I think it's absolutely ridiculous to look upon her as a saint just because she's been successful."

Not all looked upon her that way, of course. Said James Maxwell in his *Saturday Evening Post* article: "In addition to the responsibilities connected with her own show, Ruth also acts as liaison between (then) Crosley's programming and sales departments and is a member of the top planning group of the station. She unquestionably has great power within the Crosley organization, but how she uses it is often a matter of bitter debate between her admirers and detractors. She has many of both. 'She'll cut the throat of anyone who's a threat to her,' one ex-WLW employee said. 'They're scared to death of her at the station, and whatever she says goes. Personally, I think one of the reasons she's so popular is that a lot of people like to see a dictator at work as long as they're not among the victims.' Ruth indubitably exercises a firm hand over her colleagues, on camera as well as off—she has no hesitation about curtly rebuking a staff member in the middle of a broadcast if he does something which displeases her—but she maintains that such tactics are necessary to keep the show up to her standards. 'What happens on most daily shows, network as well as local,' she says, 'is that a performer has an early success, finds a formula and then coasts. As soon as I see someone letting down, I have to do something to pull things together. Everybody must have that opening-night feeling every time we go on or the show dies.' "

Men, it seems, were forever trying to take Ruth Lyons apart to see what makes her tick. Trouble is, it couldn't be done. Men will forever be men and women—allowing for Women's Lib—will, one hopes, forever be women.

Mary Wood, thus, can look at the *50/50 Club* in the days of Ruth Lyons and see something us guys would never see, or if we saw, we might never have considered.

"Women," said Mary Wood, "identified strongly with Ruth. I remember when she got her first fur coat. She wore it on the show and everybody in the audience was delighted. They actually cheered. She could finally afford a mink."

"And," said Elsa Sule, "Miss Lyons said on the air that day that she had been awake for three solid nights trying to decide whether to sink money into the fur coat. It was a terrible amount of money and she kept thinking of all the other things that could be done with the dollars. She worried—and everybody worried along with her."

"You know," said Mary Wood, "she absolutely—totally —identified with her audience, even the way she spoke. God knows, as far as diction was concerned, she would never play a role in Shakespeare."

"But she was grammatically good," said Elsa Sule. "That was one thing she was careful about."

"Not always," grinned Mary. "Every now and then she would say 'different than' instead of 'different from' and I would call her and raise hell."

"But about the fur coat?" I said.

"It was brown and lovely and dark," said Elsa. "She tried it on. All of us in the office voted whether she could keep it or not. Then, her studio audience voted."

"You see," said Mary, "Ruth was smart. She shared everything—well, almost everything with her audience. Like, whether or not she should spend the money on the coat, as well as every emotion every woman would have about her first fur coat. She gave her audience a great many

[155]

things to think about. The reason I say she had the first talk show on television is that she *talked* about everything, herself, the books she'd read, the celebrities who would appear, all of it. She *really* talked about things. With guests she didn't ask things like where they had been or where they were going. She would get their opinions on things. She couldn't abide the 'straight' interview."

"For instance," said Elsa, "there was the time Henry Cabot Lodge came on the *50/50 Club*. Two days before he got there, Secret Service men and television experts arrived to work out the format. They decided where Mr. Lodge would sit, which camera shots would be used, and which questions would be asked. We got many instructions. Miss Lyons listened to them all, carefully and politely. When Mr. Lodge came on the program things didn't go as planned. For one thing, he's too nice. Quite charming. Mrs. Lodge who was with him was excited; she had never seen her husband on color television before. Anyway, when Mr. Lodge came on, the plans the experts had made went skittering. He decided, along with Miss Lyons, it would be more fun to rock in the rocking chair than sit in the straight one his experts had suggested. He and Miss Lyons sat and rocked and talked and had a ball. She didn't ask any of the questions she was supposed to ask. What the viewers got was a good conversation."

"That was the first time," said Mary, "that Mr. Lodge had been seen on television as a human being. This was the way Ruth did things. They didn't talk about the major issues of the campaign. They talked about a great many things, but none of those. The result was, all the other politicians wanted equal time . . ."

A diverse lady was Miss Lyons. Her likes, she once wrote,

"are early American furniture, old newspapers and magazines, chocolate ice cream, an open fire, traveling anywhere, playing bridge, old people, ships, babies, honest opinions, and, like any other woman, millions of bracelets. I heartily dislike intolerance, injustice in any form, women over eighteen who try to be coy, pomposity, discrimination, licorice and mice. I love music by Tchaikovsky, Puccini, Bach, Rodgers and Hammerstein (and especially the score of *The King and I*.) I have met and especially liked, among many other people, the late General George Marshall; counted the late Robert Taft as a warm personal friend; enjoyed interviews with the late Dr. Nelson Glueck, writer and archaeologist and president of Cincinnati's Hebrew Union College; Eva Gabor; Jack Webb; Roger Smith, star of *77 Sunset Strip*; Rod Serling, one of my most successful personal friends; Carol Channing; Liberace; Eydie Gormé, and Jack E. Leonard—just to mention a few. I would like to have met Dr. Albert Schweitzer, Joseph Welch, Sir Winston Churchill, Clark Gable, President Dwight Eisenhower, and Adlai Stevenson. I would love best to revisit Paris; Amsterdam; New York; Lucerne, Switzerland; Hawaii; and New Orleans—in that order. I like best the writings of Shakespeare, Tolstoi, James Michener and Pearl Buck. My unsatisfied ambitions are to learn to tap dance, be a professional photographer, and to shoot at least an eighty in golf. . ."

How did she get to be called "Mother"? Said Miss Lyons, "Somewhere along the line, I know not where, the nickname 'Mother' was bestowed on me. It seems everyone calls me 'Mother'—newspaper columnists, truck and taxi drivers, my boss and my co-workers, and even people I don't know."

[157]

But Elsa Sule called her *Miss Lyons*.

"I called her *Ruth* once," Elsa admitted. "We were playing bridge. I probably trumped her ace. So I went back to calling her Miss Lyons."

"Ruth always said that without Elsa, she could never have run the *50/50 Club*," said Mary Wood. "Elsa is the most stable of them all. She knows more. She remembers more. And she eases away more trouble spots than anyone else."

"What specifically did you ease?" I said.

"Nothing," said Elsa, grinning. "But it sounds beautiful, Mary. Just keep talking. I just think it's remarkable that I haven't been fired years before. I don't think I've done anything to *be* fired for, but you know how things are in broadcasting. But about Miss Lyons and today's audience: I think she'd have made it with the younger generation. She has this gift of communication and identification with her audience. This is the reason Jack Parr made it. This is the reason Arthur Godfrey made it. This is the reason anybody truly great in the medium has made it. You've got to identify, stimulate, and make them *think*. It's perhaps television's equivalent to charisma on the stage, charisma that Al Jolson had. I hear he had it. I never saw him. I was too young," she concluded impishly.

"Dean Martin has it," said Mary Wood. "And Frank Sinatra."

"Paul Dixon has it," said Elsa. "And don't forget Bob Braun."

"Is television," I said, "perhaps nothing more than an oversimplified marketing device?"

Mary Wood answered fast. "I'm a marketing device,

too," she said. "Forgive me but I've got a very high reader-ship. I think it's because I've been hanging in there so long. I'm a commercial type—or, at least my column is. So are your books. So are churches when you think about it. But, as Ruth did, we've got to have appeal to the public and have rapport with them or forget it."

"When I first started working for Miss Lyons," said Elsa, "I was scared to death of her and couldn't be myself. I was completely in awe of her. I worked for her for a year before I could relax. I guess that's why I never called her anything but Miss Lyons. Anyway, she has a thing about this. She was taught when she was a girl that people who are older—even by a only a year—should be called *Mr.* or *Mrs.* or even *Uncle*, but that you should never call them by their first names. She very rarely called Mr. Dunville by his first name of Bob. Mr. Shouse, to her, was always *Mr.* Shouse. And when we went to New York she called Victor Emanuel, *Mr.* Emanuel. She had a real big thing about this. Oh sometimes I called her *Boss Lady* or *Miss L.*"

"Did you ever quarrel with her?" I said.

"Constantly," beamed Elsa. "We'd actually scream at one another. About politics. About anything, really. But I never would quarrel with her about the operation of her office. We only quarreled about the big issues—and she wouldn't give in and neither would I. One beautiful thing about Miss Lyons is, she didn't want to be surrounded by people who *yessed* her. She didn't want people just to agree with her to get along. She loved a good fight. Listen, she and I had some marvelous fights over bridge, like, should she have led the spade. Big screaming arguments. This is

[159]

what she wanted. She didn't want agreement for the sake of agreement. If someone agreed with her and she thought they didn't mean it, she got mad."

"And the next day?"

"No grudges. She didn't hold grudges."

Her loyalty to her staff, and even those at WLW-Television who were not directly connected with the 50/50 *Club* staff, was a beautiful thing to behold. She was the wailing wall for all who were in trouble. The way she felt was, the staff was her family—and as "mother," she looked out after them. If someone dickering for a raise that was deserved didn't get enough, she saw to it that the person did. If someone had personal problems and told her, she knocked herself out trying to solve them. She was also a strong influence on WLW-Television itself. She would encourage them to try new shows and new talent. If the show or the talent succeeded, great. If not, nothing ventured, nothing gained.

The loyalty worked both ways, too—in and out of the station itself. Said Mary Wood, "For many, many years L. B. Wilson—who put WCKY on the air, was one of this area's finest men, and had a heart bigger than human hearts can be—had always wanted to hire Ruth Lyons, Periodically, she would get a call from him, sounding her out. Well, then for awhile she was made program director at WLWT, a job she didn't want at all because she had no time for it. But since back then no one knew anything about television and she seemed to know the most she was given the job anyway. She held the position awhile and quickly as possible got rid of it. I ran the announcement in my column that Ruth was no longer WLWT's program director. L. B. Wilson was on the telephone right away.

'Listen, Ruth,' he said full of generosity and love for the lady, 'You come right down here and go to work. They can't fire you. You'll always have a place on my station. Just name your price.' When she said, 'But, Mr. Wilson, I didn't *want* to be program director, I—' he refused to believe her. It took several of us to convince him that no one had really hurt Ruth. Those are the kind of friends she has in and out of the business."

Remember when Willie Thall was the sidekick on the Ruth Lyons program? Great and talented guy. James Maxwell wrote that "Willie had been with Ruth for seven years when he left (in 1957) to begin his own show on WKRC-TV, Cincinnati. Since his departure, Ruth has selected no full-time replacement, although a number of males, including singers Frank Parker and Dick Noel, have appeared as guests. Any man who takes over Willie's assignment on a permanent basis is likely to find the job extremely demanding. Because the show is completely devoid of script or even predetermined subject matter, and the format is exactly what comes to Ruth's mind when she is before the cameras, he must have the mobility of a broken-field runner, the timing of a trapeze performer and the psychic perception of a Dunninger." Note: Bob Braun met all these needs and in addition could sing—and had dimples! "Willie's role in the show—the female-dominated, affable but bumbling male—was one which has become as standard in radio and television as the low comic in Shakespeare's plays."

But Willie Thall left—and that, for Ruth Lyons, was a sad and rather personal loss. Said Mary Wood, "Willie and Ruth had this great rapport. They played against each other so beautifully. But Willie was offered a show of his own at WKRC-TV and he left. Ruth was really heartbroken. She

[161]

couldn't understand it. She cried. Then Peter Grant came along. Peter worked with Ruth till he retired, alternating days with Bob Braun. Neither one of them tried to be another Willie Thall. Willie Thall was himself. So were they. But until Pete retired, Ruth had decided she was never going to have just one man on the show with her. However, Bob filled the bill and bit by bit, they developed their own rapport. Ruth had this knack, you see, of bringing people out of themselves. Marian Spelman was about the shyest girl who ever lived until she started working with Ruth. She had this tremendous sense of humor, but only Marian's closest friend ever knew it until Ruth brought it out. The same was true with Bert Farber and Cliff Lash. Ruth brought both of them out. This may be one of her secrets. Everybody on her show is a star. Eddie Bennett—and all the boys in the band—absolutely worshipped her. Everybody was a personality, even the audience. Hers was a family show."

"When Miss Lyons would come on," said Elsa Sule, "she was an actual *visitor* in the homes. We used to get letters from lonely little old ladies who told us they always got dressed up to watch the *50/50 Club*. The letters would say how they would put on clean dresses, comb their hair and put on a little makeup just to sit in front of the television set when Miss Lyons was visiting them.

"Which brings up the matter of the white gloves," I said.

"I just really don't remember how that started except that Miss Lyons said once that to be well-dressed one really should wear white gloves," Elsa said. "So, after that, everybody who came to the show wore white gloves. There would be all those white gloves waving when the cameras

[162]

showed the studio audience to its friends at home. Listen, I have a friend—an exceedingly intelligent gal—who called me one day to say she was coming to a 50/50 *Club* telecast and her navy blue kid gloves went much better with the outfit she was wearing. She wanted to know if she could wear the blue gloves or did she *have* to wear white ones."

"And now?"

"The show is more informal now," Elsa said. "I remember when Miss Lyons wore a hat on the air and all the ladies wore hats, too. But later, Miss Lyons stopped wearing hats. She used to be known for some of the real kooky ones she had. Matter of fact, Hedda Hopper once gave her one. A nice yellow straw. It's still in the office."

Ruth Lyons, of course, could attract hats *and* she could sell anything—anything she set her mind to, that is. She now and then sold items unintentionally, too. Once a guest commented on her perfume, asking the name of it. Ruth Lyons replied that it was her favorite, named it, and—though expensive and French—the perfume sold like crazy. In three days there was not one bottle of it left in Cincinnati, Dayton, or Columbus.

"Miss Lyons," said Elsa, "would either drive today's television producer out of his mind, because of all the new regulations, or she herself would be driven out of her mind. There are more regulations now than when she was on the air, like only so many commercials in a half hour. It would be difficult for Miss Lyons to have worked this way. She never worked under a 'tight format' at all. Under today's tight format I don't know whether she could have been as spontaneous as she was—but knowing her, she would have found a way. Luckily she was on television at the right time, but times are changing and not always for the better."

[163]

"If Ruth had a guest she didn't want to interrupt for a commercial," said Mary, "she would just say, 'Well, we have so many commercials so let's get them all out of the way first.' She would never be comfortable in a David Frost format that stops the show cold every so often. She —my God, let me tell you about one supermarket chain and Ruth Lyons! They sponsored her for years. The company changed hands, some bright executive appeared on the scene and said there was nothing to her show, so he cancelled their advertising on it. A competitor jumped in *fast*. The original chain, until then, had been 'way up there. It went shooosh!"

"Could she have sold that well today?"

Elsa shrugged. "Regulations," she said, "would have made it harder for Miss Lyons. But, as I say, she would have found a way to circumvent them."

"She had the faculty of swinging with the times," said Mary. "I watched Ruth grow in broadcasting. I could see her develop. She reads a lot and she is receptive to ideas. I think Ruth could have made it in these times because she would have been *with* these times. She was a great leveler, you know. In her own way, she broke down many prejudices. When she came back from Russia, she talked about the Russian *people*, the kind we were, not about higher echelon politics. I think if she were on today she would be doing worlds of good, establishing communication between the generations. She always loved youth. And she always loved the older ones. I think she could have made the older generation and the younger generation understand each other."

"What about her husband?" I said.

[164]

"Herman is quite liberal," said Mary. "Herman is a real revolutionist."

"How much influence did he have on Ruth Lyons?"

"A great deal!" That came from *both* Mary and Elsa. "When I first knew Miss Lyons," Elsa added, "she was a conservative Republican. Now she's a liberal Democrat. I'm the Republican who keeps fighting her. I'm a registered Democrat, that's the kind of Republican I am, but I keep fighting and on the telephone I kept telling Miss Lyons to go back to her youth and her Republican ancestors. But she paid no attention to me."

"Was she a liberal when to be a liberal was unpopular?" I said.

"Yes," said Elsa. "She was a liberal but she would not be for violence. She was for new ideas and racial equality."

"Whenever Pearl Bailey came on the show," said Mary, "she would practically be Ruth's co-hostess. Ruth was the first in television that I know of to have blacks on and not just give them a quick brushoff introduction but get to know them as people. She would talk with Pearl Bailey about her husband, her children, and her way of life. She would talk to Duke Ellington about his background, his music, *him*, himself. In other words, she wanted her audience to know these people as people and not just performers. That was Ruth's approach: people to people. This was Ruth's *thing*."

Ruth Lyons said once that "I don't believe that the average woman's only concern is with the dust cloth and getting Junior off to school on time. She cares about what is happening in her city and the rest of the world. Well, I get around a bit and I read a lot and I tell my audiences about the things that interest me. When I flip about Cincinnati cutting down the trees on Central Parkway, I flip on the air, and when I come across an article, say, on the falling birth rate in Ireland or a new wonder drug or why the electoral college is out of date, I discuss it. Women have brains, you know, and they're usually pleased when someone takes cognizance of the fact . . ."

Unlike many people with strong opinions, one observer noted, Ruth Lyons was an attentive listener, but added, "she is incapable of languid conversation, either in her home or in her office." Such attentiveness paid off handsomely for her friends in the television audience. It made her a better-than-average (understatement of the season) interviewer. For one thing, she tried never to meet her guests before she met them on camera. She felt conversation should be spontaneous.

"But," said Mary, "you must remember that she was one girl who never went on the air unprepared. If she was going to interview a writer, she would have read his book. She would be able to discuss his book intelligently. She wasn't the way some interviewers are when they mutter, 'I haven't had a chance to read your book, but. . .' Ruth would have read the book, would have formed an opinion on it, and would be ready to go into it. She is an intellectual dame. She's not a stupid woman. She would often read a book in one evening. She never asked superficial questions. She would go right to the heart of whatever the guest had to say—and make sure it was said."

"And she would listen," said Elsa. "Some interviewers ask questions and then are so busy thinking of the next question they don't hear your answer. Miss Lyons would always shut up and *listen*."

Bob Braun in his book *Here's Bob* recalls the day Arthur Simpkins appeared on the *50/50 Club* with Ruth Lyons. "When he was singing and doing his rhythmic dance," Bob wrote, "Ruth got so carried away she jumped up and began to dance with him. Need I tell you that the phones rang off the wall? People complained about her dancing with a Negro. Was Ruth mad! She did not apologize for her actions, but rather raised what-for on the next day's program to those who had phoned and written in. She won. She was deluged with mail from those who had felt she had done no wrong, which indeed she had not. Arthur is one of the finest gentlemen in show business. As a result of his appearance on Ruth's show that day, he sold more than ten thousand copies of his record album."

Also, Bob recalled Miss Lyons' visit to the governor's mansion in Columbus. "C. William O'Neill was the Governor of Ohio," Bob wrote. "He and his wife Betty had become great fans and very good friends of Ruth Lyons. When Governor and Mrs. O'Neill learned she was bringing her show to Columbus, they extended an invitation to Ruth and all her cast for lunch at the governor's mansion. We were all very excited. I had never been to the mansion or met the Governor, any governor for that matter. Governor O'Neill sent each of us an engraved invitation (I still have mine) and we thought the day would never come. But it did finally arrive. Following the program we went by motorcade to the mansion. Naturally, we were all on our good behavior. Mrs. O'Neill welcomed us along with the Governor. I can remember thinking she was very nice. I don't know what I expected, but I was certainly impressed with the fact that she could have well been my neighbor, or yours. The Governor's Mansion is in the Bexley area of

Columbus. It is a very large English-style home with lots of paneling and beamed ceilings. There is a large reception area with a family dining room to the left as you enter and a sunken living room to the right. We were received there and taken into the huge living room. Lunch was to be served in still another large room to the rear of the living room. It was what you might term in a smaller home a family room. It, too, was decorated in the same old English style. There were nearly fifty of us in the party and there was room for all of us to be seated and then some.

"Lunch was served, and I remember it was quite good. We were all very careful to use the right fork and spoon. I sat next to Mrs. O'Neill, we talked about our kids, school, motherhood, the Fourth of July, and who knows what all. Suddenly the chatter of conversation was abruptly halted when Ruth said, "Governor, why don't you use saucers with your coffee cups?" All of us sat, stunned.

" 'We don't have enough saucers to go with all these cups,' was the governor's reply. He began to laugh, so did Mrs. O'Neill. One by one, so did the rest of us. It broke the tension and made the rest of the afternoon even more enjoyable.

"The following morning Ruth told the story on her show. Are you ready for this? Saucers began flying into the Columbus Governor's Mansion. (Pun intended.) The governor was deluged with saucers of all descriptions. I am sure our visit will never be forgotten. In all, the governor received nearly ten thousand saucers. Saucers, anyone?"

Miss Lyons—Elsa has got *me* doing it—was unpredictable. There was the time her housekeeper was ill and Ruth Lyons hauled the damp laundry to the station where she had a row of ironing boards set up in the studio. While she played the organ and sang, ladies from the studio audience did her ironing for her! And her guests were unpredictable, too—thanks to her. When Eva Gabor appeared, she and Ruth Lyons "chattered away like sorority sisters at a class reunion," said one writer. When Steve Allen appeared, with such a tight schedule his manager only allowed him four minutes on the *50/50 Club*, he stayed what seemed like forever to his manager. Steve, carried away with the charm of Ruth Lyons, and vice versa, played piano, she played organ, and they "jammed" with Cliff Lash and the band. When Victor Borge appeared, he and Ruth Lyons started out with a duet on the same piano, but since the bench wasn't big enough for two, he ended up climbing down under the piano, reaching up for the keyboard.

Betty Hannah Hoffman wrote in the April 1960, *Ladies' Home Journal* that "when Ruth cries, her whole face shines wetly. When the audience starts sobbing, she trips among them trailing her flower-decked microphone and letting the fortunate ones sniff her smelling salts. Ruth's special interest includes children—especially hurt, crippled, or sick children—dogs and elderly women. 'It's their necks that get me,' Ruth explains. 'Little old ladies with narrow shoulders and stringy bent necks—they break me up.' When Denise Darcel appeared on her program, they got to discussing the zingy actress's elderly mother in France and ended up sobbing in each other's arms . . .

"When she left for Europe one year, she happened to mention on the air which train she was taking from Cincinnati. (Neither she nor her husband ever flies anywhere.) When the train carrying Ruth and her husband and daughter pulled into Springfield, Ohio, five hundred women were waiting in the pouring rain for a glimpse of their

[169]

idol. When Ruth finally appeared on the back platform, she was weeping copiously. 'Ruth's so sentimental she cries at coming attractions,' says a close friend sympathetically. 'Another thing about Ruth that clutches her audience's interest: she always feels terrible.' "

The article went on to say that Ruth Lyons' constant aches and pains were a running gag on her noon show. For a long, long time she was always at death's door, yet never actually sick—so said the article. She did, however, once break her little toe. It was, they say, not only done up in an enormous white bandage but had, in addition, red ribbons and flowers as well! Ruth Lyons said it throbbed all through the show's ninety minutes. Also, she was forever complaining about how her "miserable elbows" were always causing trouble. And always, there was advice: buy white cars. "It's the only color," she told her audience, "and besides white cars are safer."

In recalling her Cincinnati childhood Ruth Lyons once wrote that it "centered around the activities of the Presbyterian church of our neighborhood. I played the piano and later the organ, sang in the junior choir, and accompanied my father, two uncles and my grandfather in their vocal quartet. I could play tunes on the piano when I was three years old, remember melodies after hearing them only once, have always had perfect pitch. I studied piano, organ and violin and learned to play the ukulele by stringing an old tennis racket with four lengths of wrapping cord to simulate the instrument. My grandfather on my mother's side was a captain on the Ohio and Mississippi Rivers. Living on the Ohio, I loved its boats and fascinating stories— and still do. My mother was dainty, gay, old-fashioned, delightfully superstitious and gently determined. My father was an expert mathematician, witty, extravagant, and absolute putty in mother's hands. My family's greatest claim to local fame was ownership of the first phonograph in our neighborhood complete with a large collection of records by Caruso, Melba and, a bit later, the ever-popular John McCormack."

And, of course, the Ruth Lyons Christmas Fund.

"I started it," she said, "with one hospital in 1939—the Children's Hospital in Cincinnati—when I was made aware of the lack of anything in the hospitals to divert a sick child's mind from his own anxieties and pain. There were no books, no toys, no radios—nothing in the way of material things to hasten his tedious recovery. And most unfortunate of all, there was no money available to make these things possible. So, as I always do, I put the problem before my (then) radio audience, primarily to raise a fund to give hospitalized children a truly wonderful Christmas. The first year the fund raised one thousand dollars. The drive, still conducted annually, has raised nearly 6 million dollars since its inception. The children themselves have an abiding faith in this fund and there have been hundreds of wonderful stories told to us by nurses and doctors in the hospitals as to what has been accomplished in making these little ones as happy as possible while they were hospitalized. We raise this money each year by starting Christmas in October. Many Christmas songs which I have written over the years, released now in albums, have played a major part in bringing alive the Christmas spirit of giving in the hearts of our audience. These people know these songs and sing them with us, so they tell me, all year long."

How did she sum up her active life, five shows a week?

"Frantic, busy, creative, productive, frustrating, delightful, maddening," she said once, "but never dull. And when the show is over and after the many conferences and a reassuring call from long-suffering management telling me that I'm not going to be fired this time, but watch it—then I go home to be Ruth Newman . . .

"Wife to an understanding, delightfully argumentative professor of that unintelligible subject, English . . .

"Godmother to six Japanese spaniels, one Irish setter, a pale yellow canary, and a huge Persian cat . . .

"Overseer-in-name-only of a ten-room house but in reality slave to Pauline and Callie, our two devoted housekeepers, who tell me what to do . . .

"And most of all—to be *myself*, free to read, watch every television show I can work in, write some new tunes, eat, talk and talk and talk with Herman . . . sit quietly by the fire and be thankful that 'life can be a lovely way of living' —and so to bed."

"That was Ruth Lyons?" I said to Mary and Elsa.

They both nodded.

"What will you write of Candy?" one of them said.

"Only that she was beautiful and she was loved," I said.

Because Candy, short for Candace, was the only child of Mr. and Mrs. Herman Newman. They loved her dearly. She is no longer among us.

The memory of her is too fragile to run through this typewriter of mine.

Okay?

Paul Dixon, who loved Ruth Lyons, too, did not know how to write of her in his book, *Paul Baby*. "Ruth," he wrote, "how can I write about you and what can I say? I thought first of kidding about how 'Paul's Pot' helped raise funds for the Christmas Fund. All the women bombarded me with pennies as I sang. But I can't really kid about that. The Christmas Fund is a serious affair.

"What are you like when the cameras are off? The women of your audience already know, Ruth, because they have always known, haven't they? Wherever you are—at home now or when you were rocking in your chair here at the station—you were the only thing you could ever be: *yourself*. And, Ruth, that's good enough for me and the thousands of women out there who love you, too.

"The thousand and one kindnesses you have shown me flash before me as I write this. When I was in the hospital, you were there—so *many* times! And you made certain that I wasn't forgotten—and by a thousand little selfless acts, you made me feel better. Yet, to list these acts here would seem impolite, an invasion of the privacy you have rightfully earned. But let me say only this publicly: thank you. *Thank you!*

"Is it true you're no longer on the air, Ruth? I know it is true but I can't conceive of it. WLW-Television *without* a Ruth Lyons? Impossible. That would be the same as having the sky without stars or the world without love. Ruth, you made this place what it is today. You personally created the friendly atmosphere we now enjoy. Because you were, we can be. I'm saying this badly but you understand, don't you, Ruth. You've always understood. So how can I presume to say that when the tally lights went off and your show was over for the day, you changed? All I know as I write this is I miss you and that I am not alone. You are missed by everyone. Do you remember that lonely little ballad called 'Have I Stayed Too Long at the Fair?' It tells of a girl who wanders about the silent fairgrounds after the clowns have left, the crowds have vanished, and the ferris

[173]

wheel has stopped running. I remember one day one of the girls sang that song on your show. And I remember that you commented, with a kind of melancholy, that perhaps you, too, had stayed too long at the fair. And a few days later, Ruth, you got a letter that said it better than I could have ever said it. The letter said simply: 'Miss Lyons, don't worry about staying too long at the fair. Stay as long as you want. Because when you leave, the fair will be over . . .'"

"When Candy was learning to walk," Ruth Lyons once wrote, "along came a strange new Circe, activated by a small snap-on switch, full of more wiles and enchantments than any pony-tailed Lorelei. Her name was television . . ."

And her other name was Ruth Lyons.

BOB BRAUN, as any post-pubescent female within whistling distance of WLW-Television can tell you better than I, is a most handsome lad. His place of residence on the tube is the *50/50 Club*, once the front porch of Ruth Lyons, but she did her show her way, he does his his way, both agree this is best, and so do all the lovely ladies in attendance each day at noon. Bob, unlike Ruth, is not a local personality. He came here from out of state to go into show business. He came from Ludlow, Kentucky, just across the river from Cincinnati, a few minutes away from our downtown area if, that is, one doesn't get hung up in Covington.

Herewith is issued the same disclaimer that must be issued where Paul Dixon is also concerned. To write about Bob Braun in a detached manner, as one might look at a chest X-ray of a stranger or a house you don't wish to buy, is impossible for me. As in the case of Paul Baby, I happen to be fond of Bob Braun and look upon him as a friend. He is the first lifeguard I ever felt this way about. And he *did* used to be a lifeguard at Coney Island, sitting up there on that high wooden chair, twirling his whistle, flexing his muscles, showing his teeth, combing his hair, doing headstands when in the mood, and—well, you know how lifeguards do. They do everything but get wet.

Like Dixon, Braun came to WLW-Television after getting a start under WCPO-TV's Mort Watters who had so much to do with making Cincinnati a number one television town insofar as "live" television went. I first met Bob at the old WCPO-TV studios on Symmes Street when he returned from the military. A talented crew had been assembled in those days on Symmes Street, some more talented than the others, but of them all Bob had the most curls. Glenn Ryle, now Skipper Ryle at WKRC-TV, was a staff announcer at WCPO-TV then. Dotty Mack was there. So was Colin Male, a private eye from Buffalo who drifted into town and got a job as an announcer, later to go west to Hollywood where he now can be seen acting in many of the situation comedies as well as peddling products via national commercials. Jim Stacey was there, so were Al Lewis and Wanda who are *still* there, and in those wild and freewheeling days of television we seemed to have more weather girls than we had weather. Al Shottelkotte, on the other hand, had yet to arrive. Walt Phillips was doing a shift on WCPO-Radio (now WUBE) and also, with Jana Demas, doing a two-hour live "something" (I directed it but could never figure what it was) on Saturday afternoon on WCPO-TV. And always, waiting in the wings, was Harris Rosedale and a clutch of spindly-legged urchins wearing chiffon, spangles, lipstick, and tap shoes, every one a Shirley Temple reincarnate, ready to do the time-step as best they could,

[176]

waiting for stardom to strike. WLWT, in those days, had Ruth Lyons. WCPO-TV, in competition, had Paul Dixon, urchins doing tap routines, and Uncle Al forever on his knees among the sticky-finger set. It was into this noisy and merry and hectic melange that Bob Braun, fresh from the military, returned to WCPO-TV and his old job.

Before going off to the military, Bob Braun had run camera at WCPO-TV for the *Paul Dixon Show*. Even before then he had been on television. The name of the station was W8XCT, the forerunner of WLWT, Cincinnati. He appeared on a program whose master of ceremonies was—of all people—the aforementioned Harris Rosedale. But this stint did not lead him to WCPO-TV. Sitting on the marquee of a theater in Cincinnati did. As a promotion stunt for the movie *Blue Lagoon* he stayed on the marquee for a week, the marquee being decked out with palm trees, grass, and other tropical island devices. Ed Weston, program director of WCPO-TV, hired Bob, figuring that anyone who could survive atop a theater marquee for a week might not hold out for a high salary. At WCPO-TV, Bob sang, worked props, ran camera, and—when not involved with such show business activities—swept out the studios. At one time he also had a program called *Uncle Bob Reads the Sunday Comics*, which he would have anyway. He also sang on *Bride to Be*. Says Bob in his book *Here's Bob:*

"At one point in each show I would serenade the bride with a love song. One of the show's sponsors was Wolf's Bakery, owned by the dad of Dave Wolf, a friend of mine. I think that may have had more than a small part in my getting a job." After the military stint, Bob came back to WCPO-TV to announce the morning shift as well as direct *The Uncle Al Show*. Then came *Pantomime Hit Parade* with Dotty Mack and Colin Male. Then came a shot at Arthur Gordfrey's Talent Scouts (he won because he wowed 'em) and then came, as it must to all men, the parting of the ways. Bob and WCPO-TV parted, amiably, but nonetheless parted.

Bob doesn't change much through the years. One wishes, me being the one, that he would grow—and *look*—older as the rest of us have done. He doesn't. His youthfulness has to do with push-ups, bar bells, or something silly like that. He is still the masculine animal he was when he was perched atop the wood bench at Coney Island, doing life-saving things. And he—himself—is still the same. A most cheerful and a most practical guy. A hard worker, too. He does his show well because he does his homework well.

He has the charming ability to make the small print on the packages of products read like something William Shakespeare or Rod McKuen cranked out as copywriters. His mind, frankly, amazes me. Without the use of idiot boards, except as occasional reminders, he rips off one commercial after another, in his own style, but almost exactly as written, word for word, comma for comma. He must have committed to memory more than a thousand commercials, any one of which he could do verbatim and ad lib at the drop of the hat he doesn't wear. Now and then, but actually seldom, he does err, tossing out the wrong fact or color or benefit.

Says Elsa Sule, who has been with WLW for seventy-eight years and is now the gal in charge of the commercials on Bob's show, "There is a difference between working for Bob and working for Miss Lyons as I did. Although neither hold grudges—both are too big for anything as childish as that—Bob can get furious fast. But he gets over it just as fast. He's a perfectionist and, though the program may seem casual to those watching at home, he constantly strives for perfection in everything, driving himself harder than he would ever think of driving any of the rest of us. But he hates to be contradicted on the air. Miss Lyons might be doing a commercial and get something backwards and if she did, she wanted us to correct her then and there. That's how she wanted it and that's how she told us to do it. But Bob is different. He doesn't want to be corrected on the air. He wants to be corrected off the air. And then next day, or when he's back on camera again, he will correct the error himself, blaming himself in front of the viewers. He doesn't pass the buck. As far as he's concerned, the buck stops with him. It's just that he gets so involved with guests and commercials and the *movement* of the show, he doesn't want to be interrupted by someone yelling in. Different people do things different ways. He's not Miss Lyons, Miss Lyons is not Bob—and both are the better for each."

Added Elsa, "Bob is wonderful, really. When he is having a good time, you can be sure it's going to be a good show. If he enjoys it, everybody else—the viewers, the control room, all of us—enjoy it, too. And this feeds back to him, this enjoyment, and the show just keeps building so you hate to see the end of the show arrive."

Bob Braun, in one sense, *inherited* his present show and much of his present audience. He inherited the band, the prop boys, a clutch of secretaries, and dibs on the factory that turns out white gloves. We'll go into the matter of his inheritance later on in this chapter, but for the moment let us look at Bob Braun himself. Just as

Paul Dixon is and Ruth Lyons was, Bob Braun can be considered a kind of one-man industry. He is the product and the maker of the product offered each day at noon. He has as Dixon does and Miss Lyons did a tremendous responsibility which, on camera, he must carry lightly.

As the majordomo for the ninety minutes the program is on the air, he must keep the program paced properly. After all, this is live television like Mother used to make and no editor snipping tape can edit it into perfection. Each and every day when the red tally lights of the cameras come on Bob Braun—and crew—get one chance and one chance only—to put together the ninety-minute program. The pacing of it, as suggested, rests on Bob's shoulders. If the program falters—say, a guest turns out to be a dog—the task of picking up the momentum lies with Bob. He can't call for help. He can't stop and start over. This is the wonder—and the agony—of live television. And because he is good at pacing, this is the beauty of Bob Braun. He makes live television, which is exhausting, look like child's play. The true art, someone once said, is in the concealment of art. Bob, in this manner, is a true artist.

But his responsibilities do not begin and end with the start and end of the program. Once the program is over, he, like Dixon, reverts somewhat exhausted to what might be properly termed "the business world." His office would make any major executive in any major industry look with awe. But why shouldn't it be big and beautiful and grandiose? Look at the visitors who daily sit across the desk from him.

One day might find the president of a company whose product is being advertised on the program. Listen, when

Bob Metzger loaded! WLWT's first newsmen covered radio as well as television

Left to Right: Tom McGuire, Tony Randall, and Bob Atkins—WLWT
anchormen of *all* events
Robert Metzger

Veteran broadcaster Jack Lescoulie hosts many of Avco
Broadcasting's documentaries. Here Jack visits the University
of Cincinnati campus to interview students for *Freshman Fantasy*.
Accompanying Jack is Avco Broadcasting's Director of Special
Projects Don Dunkel, and skilled cinematographer Bill Leslie

Jack Lescoulie and Rosemary Kelly telecasting St. Patrick's Day Parade
Robert Metzger

Walter Scarborough, one of the many 'Round-the-clock newsmen' at Avco
Broadcasting   *Robert Metzger*

Each summer Avco Broadcasting transports casts, crews and technical
equipment to Columbus, Ohio, where it originates all of its programs live
from the Ohio State Fair. Avco's participation has helped to make
the Ohio fair the largest in the nation

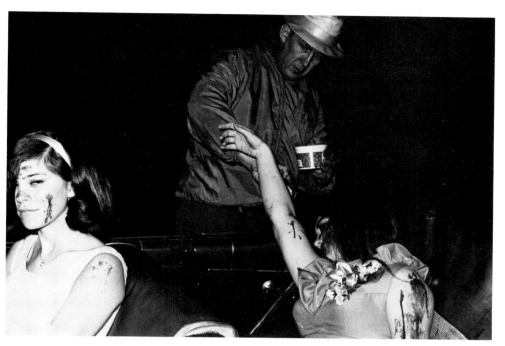

Getting cast "dolled up" for WLW's documentary *The Last Prom*

Robert Metzger

Joe Lewin, right, shooting a WLW television documentary on the Ohio
River

Robert Metzger

David McCoy on location for an Avco Broadcasting Television Special
Robert Metzger

Shooting an Avco Broadcasting documentary on the Appalachian poor

Phil Donahue, seen nationally, considers himself more a newsman than entertainer   *Robert Metzger*

Phil Donahue welcomes superstar Glen Campbell to his weekday program

Paul Dixon with his two most famous symbols. His binoculars (with which he examines Kneesville each morning) and his seltzer bottle. ("How many of you girls took a bath this morning?") The Paul Dixon Show is ninety minutes of such diverse activities as . . .

Seeing Bonnie Lou in her original Dixon Show costume . . .

Awarding garters to Brides-to-Be . . .

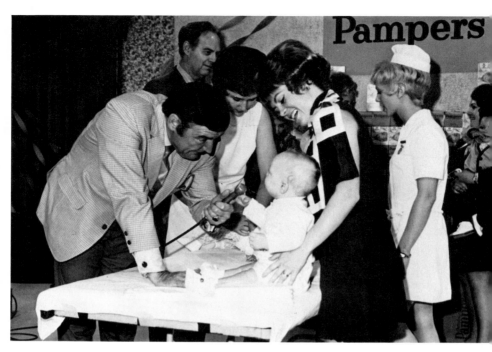

Losing verbal battles with babies . . .

And, upon occasion, his blue serge aplomb . . .

Tossing Colleen Sharp into the hopper . . .

. . . and staging weddings for rubber chickens.

The Hot Pants Show. All members of the cast, crew, and studio audience were required to wear the short shorts to the program!

Bob Braun arrives some mornings with a car load

Rehearses with the 50/50 *Club* Band

Autographs copies of his book

With David McCoy, meets a Republican

With Marian Spelman, meets a Democrat

And meets Paul Lynde on his own

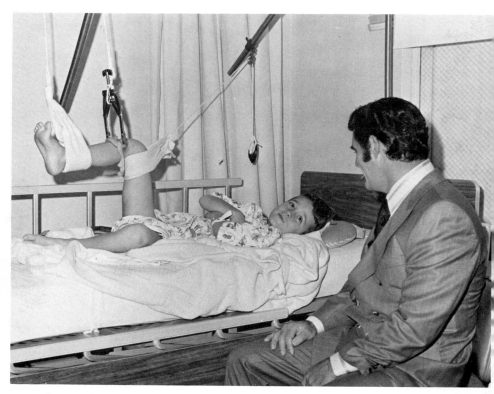

After work? Visits hospitals and the kids who have benefited from The Ruth Lyons Christmas Fund

you chat with company presidents you don't chat with them in broom closets, do you? The same day might find, in conference gathered, high officials from Avco Television. I'll say that another way: officials high in the ranks of Avco Television. They might be planning a business assault on New York City in which Bob Braun's presence might or might not be required. The same day in his office might find network television stars, bosomy movie stars hustling their latest flick, writers, baseball stars—you name it, every category. And roaming in and out will be Cliff Lash, Marian Spelman, and all the rest—secretaries, shoeshine boys, television producers, and public relations men. Frankly, Bob Braun needs a big office. At times it is as crowded as Grand Central Station. There is, indeed, hardly room for Bob himself. He can hardly sneak his dimples in.

The real test of a guy whose face is as well known as any you might see on the tube is what kind of guy is he when he's tooting down the street alone in his car. He has owned cars the way Izzy Kadetz owns matzoh. Well, I don't know about you, but I do know about Bob. Some men, in the public eyes, toot along, hoping no one sees them for fear the person will ask a favor. Not Bob Braun. With a blast of the car horn, he gets your attention and waves with true friendliness and—at times, sad thought— with a kind of true loneliness, as if you are the last friend he has in the world. Some people, as the result of television exposure, have been dehumanized. But no one can say that about Bob. He is as real as the kid he was in Ludlow, Kentucky—and you can't get any more *real* than that!

My sister, who looks somewhat like me, once was in New York, walking along Broadway. Bob Braun had never met her. But with a wild shout and a wild wave, he asked

[181]

if she was my sister and they spent ten minutes—pedestrians muttering mutters at them—blocking sidewalk traffic and yacking. Point is, Bob Braun who doesn't have to do things like that nonetheless *does* them. In other words, the smiles he smiles at the viewers are not phony smiles. They are not phony because he himself is not a phony; and, listen, there are a lot of phonies in the television business. Ask any announcer, out of a job and pounding the pavement, who his real friends are.

There is much about Bob Braun that he does not wish to publicize but, forgive me or not, I will toss a few of them at you here. Once Leo Underhill, a fictional person who exists only in the imagination of bartenders, was fired from his job at one of the local stations. One of the first calls he got, one of the few calls he got, was from Bob Braun.

"Leo, what can I do? How can I help you? Want me to call any of the stations or talk to anybody here at WLW?"

On the other hand, when Leo Underhill, then pounding the pavement, contacted those he considered to be his friends, they said warily into the telephone:

"Leo? Leo who?"

Mary Wood, writing in the *Cincinnati Post & Times-Star* did an excellent profile of Bob Braun awhile back. "Bob and Wray Jean Braun," she wrote, "live in a charming spacious French country house in a beautiful wooded area of Mount Airy. It's their dream home which they built over a year ago, and Bob gives Wray Jean all the credit for the tasteful way in which it is decorated.

" 'Wray Jean just seems to have been born with good taste,' Bob said. 'She has a great color sense.'

"The Brauns have three attractive children—Rob, Doug,

and Lissa who looks just like Poppa even to the dimples.

" 'We're bringing up our children to be aware of what's going on around them,' Bob said. 'They go to public school, play with the neighborhood children and aren't at all impressed because I'm on television. We're very open with our children and try to answer any question they ask.'

"Lissa lost a tooth the other day and the Tooth Fairy left fifty cents under her pillow.

" 'It seems to me the Tooth Fairy rates have gone up since I was a kid,' laughed Wray Jean. 'I seem to remember just getting a quarter.' "

"A few of Bob's favorite guests are Adela Rogers St. John—'You've got to be on your toes with her'—General Lewis Walt whom Bob calls the 'most compassionate man I've ever met,' and Braun's all-time favorite, Erroll Garner.

" 'A good guest sparks me and the show and I love to get that kind,' Bob explained. 'With a good person, you get under the show business facade and come up with a warm interview.'

"Bob's aim on the *50/50 Club* is to keep the show elastic and move with the times. Since they're giving away twice as many American flags on the show these days, Bob figures the audience is getting younger.

" 'When Ruby Wright retired, we looked for new talent,' said Bob. 'Marian Spelman found Bob Reider at the University of Cincinnati. He's a versatile young talent who sings and also plays guitar with the Symphony Orchestra. Randy Weidner is fresh out of the army and the closest thing we have to a rock singer.'

"What turns Bob on?

" 'People,' he replied. 'I love to be in contact with the

[183]

studio audience and I love meeting people when I go out to make personal appearances. My pet peeve is with show business people who spend their lives trying to achieve success, then complain about being bothered by their fans. I still get a thrill whenever I am asked for my autograph." '

"Wray Jean says that her marriage to Bob has never been dull. She added, 'Bob has high highs and low lows. When he has his lows, I listen and keep my mouth shut until it blows over.'

"I might point out," Mary Wood concludes, "that Bob was really lucky when he married Wray Jean. She is not only a lovely-looking young woman, she has a lot of common sense in that pretty head."

Bob Braun arrived on January 27, 1967 as host of the 50/50 Club by a most circuitous route. That was the day that Ruth Lyons, of course, announced her retirement from television and suggested that Bob take over the chores. "It was," she wrote once, "a most difficult task for Bob. He had shown, however, great strength and courage many times during the months preceding my retirement. And I knew he could be successful. Which he is. Of greatest importance to me, Bob has successfully raised the Christmas Fund each year for the hospitals throughout the area. So what more can I say, except to wish Bob, his lovely family, and the entire cast of the 50/50 Club every good thing possible?" Yes, Bob had inherited the 50/50 Club lock, stock, and barrel from the master of them all, Ruth Lyons.

Bob has said of Ruth Lyons that, "Working with her was one of life's great experiences. She was the master of doing shows like the 50/50 Club. It seemed as if she had a sixth sense about how the studio audience would react each day. Ruth would work an audience like an orchestra, playing all the parts. If there was a character of some sort in the audience, she would pick him out as if she had built-in radar helping her find him." Bob first appeared on the noon show with Ruth Lyons after Willie Thall had left. Miss Lyons wanted no one person (she had been, and still is, terribly fond of wonderful Willie Thall) so she divided the chores between Peter Grant and Bob Braun. One day one would be there, the next day the other. As soon as Bob started singing regularly on her show, he started making personal appearances because, it seemed, suddenly he was in demand.

There have been in Bob Braun's life at WLW-Television many moments, any one of which would have been momentous enough to last the rest of us a lifetime. First, there was the possibility of his own show, that early evening thing before the news. He was eager for this, reasonably so. When John Murphy offered him the time slot, he told Bob to think it over, but Bob who had been thinking of a show of his own all his life really didn't need much time to think. Said Bob, "I was hardly able to contain myself. I told Mr. Murphy simply that if he thought I could do it, that was good enough for me."

The dimpled performer organized his show with the care one plans spending one's life's savings. Chet Lishawa was the producer. The band started first with Frankie Brown, a fabulous musician besides being a nice guy, his only hangup being that he knows Dee Felice. Gene Wilson was established at the electric guitar. The drummer was Jimmy Seward. Mike Andres was the utility man, playing saxophone, flute, and clarinet. For piano Teddy Rakel, then staff arranger at WLW, was selected. Teddy Rakel is the perennially young and puckish-looking pianoman who, years before, wowed the beer-drinking set at Danny's Musical Bar out on Reading Road. The Teddy Raymore Trio, as then constituted, was something else. Teddy Rakel, whom I have never met, I have met many times via his music. Beautiful, beautiful. The point: Bob Braun collected a good musical group. Rosemary Kelly was assigned to help out Bob Braun on his afternoon stint and Nick Clooney, later to take over the chores with Vivienne Della Chiesa, was around, wondering where his pretty sisters were. Everything was ready, set to go.

"About the middle of December (before the show went on the air)," Bob recalled, "Ruth and I had a long talk concerning the new program. She began by asking me how I felt about doing it. In retrospect I really feel that she was worried about my going into that particular time slot. I was to leave her program in January when my new show was to premier. She told me she just did not feel up to breaking in a new assistant at that stage of the game. I told her that I would be glad to continue a couple of days a week to assist her if she preferred, at least until she felt comfortable with someone else. . . ."

On January 23, 1967, *The Bob Braun Show* went on the air.

Simply put, it was a success.

Two days later, while Bob was in the studio rehearsing one of his songs with the band, Mickey Fisher came in and said, "Bobby, Miss Lyons would like to see you in her office."

Bob went right in and, as he wrote in his book *Here's Bob*, "What took place in the next few minutes was to alter the lives of many people." That could have easily been the understatement of the year. It altered the lives of thousands upon thousands of viewers in the midwest. When Bob walked into her office, Ruth Lyons told him:

"Today was my last show, Bobby."

You wonder about moments, don't you? Looking back, I wonder about Bob then. He had to return to the studio to do his show, pretending that nothing had happened. The announcement would be made later. He could say nothing. The only others who were in on the news that Ruth Lyons was retiring were John Murphy, Walter Bartlett, and several girls in her office. As far as the rest of the world knew, Ruth Lyons was forever. The rest of the world didn't know that Ruth Lyons—however indestructible— was also only human. The rest of the world didn't know that for her the show—and a way of life for her and all her viewers—was over. Yet, there sat Bob Braun on the set of his show, yacking with Rosemary Kelly, and all the while torn up inside with the sad news he had just heard.

"I was in no mood at this point to do any show," Bob wrote, "but I did. But by contrast to a couple of days before, how long that hour and a half was that day. Of course, I could not mention anything about Ruth's decision on the air for it was not to be made public. I had not even officially heard it from the company at this point, but judging from the way Ruth told me, her decision was definite and her mind made up. All during the show, my mind was filled with other thoughts: What was to happen? Do I drop my new *Bob Braun Show* and take over the job of hosting the *50/50 Club?* Could I? Which was worse, four o'clock opposite Mike Douglas or trying to follow the success of this great lady? Would her audience accept me as the permanent host? Sure, they had as a substitute, but this

[187]

was different. What about the cast of *The Bob Braun Show?* They needed their jobs, too. They all had high hopes for the success of the new program. Did I just say, 'Sorry about that, I've found something better'? Would I be better off building my own show rather than trying to hold on to those who loved Ruth? I was thinking all these things . . .''

The decision, in one way, was not Bob Braun's to make. Television; for better or for worse, is more than the people like Braun and Dixon and Donahue who appear with regularity—and charm—in your living rooms. Television is all the other people involved in the industry—and it is the industry itself. True, talent can and does make decisions but only those decisions which are within their province to make and which they have been delegated to make. In the case of the *50/50 Club*—in reality, a major investment—the decision was a management one. When Walter Bartlett, senior vice president, read on the *50/50 Club* the retirement letter that Ruth Lyons had written, one part caught Bob Braun by surprise. Bartlett is responsible for all Avco-Television everywhere, the big problems and the little ones. But this was one of his biggest. Bob listened in wonderment as Mr. Bartlett read:

". . . Bobby [so went the letter Ruth Lyons wrote] has been a strong right arm to me for many years and on many occasions. During the last year he did a wonderful job on *50/50 Club*. I feel he is the only one who could continue the traditions and standards that you have all come to expect from us on the *50/50 Club* in the past. I know you will give Bobby the same kind reception given me . . ."

And *that* was *that.*

Bartlett then read a message from Avco President John Murphy which said to Bob, "We have long recognized your many talents and feel confident that in your hands *50/50 Club* will continue to be an area-wide institution for noontime listening and viewing. Please advise the staff and cast of the show—Bonnie Lou, Marian Spelman, Ruby Wright, Colleen Sharp, Peter Grant, Nick Clooney, and Cliff Lash and the orchestra, that we want them to continue with you on the *50/50 Club*."

And, as they say around WLW, when John Murphy says this is the way he would like things, you'd better believe that is the way things will be.

Well, that seems like only yesterday, but since then, the *50/50 Club* has evolved, slowly, from what it was when Ruth Lyons was there to what it is now that Bob Braun is there. Bob could no more be expected to do the kind of show Ruth Lyons did than he could someday be expected to be bald. Ruth Lyons did her show her way. She was alone in the mastery of that show. Now Bob Braun offers another kind—his own kind—of mastering. And the audiences are there. The sponsors are there. How else can a show be measured?

Many guests have sat and chatted with Bob Braun, an excellent interviewer who does his homework. Former Governor James B. Rhodes has been on the *50/50 Club* so much he is technically listed as the executive producer. Perry Como has appeared. So has Bob Hope. And so has Virginia Payne who played "Ma Perkins." People—in the news—from all walks of life have walked out on the stage to chat with Braun. For instance, there was Oleg Cassini. Add Lawrence Welk. Rowan and Martin have appeared. Also: Pat O'Brien, Peter Nero, Ed Ames, Merv Griffin, Roger Williams, José Iturbi, Guy Lombardo, and—Braun's good friend—Dick Clark.

Says Bob in his book, "Television today is a far cry from what I first knew twenty years ago when I began my career in the crazy medium of illustrated radio. At first people were fascinated by the fact that a picture had actually come through the air and into their homes. Today, they want to look closely at the picture to see what it is, to hear what is said. Each day we are on television is a new challenge . . ."

Yes, and with people like Bob Braun around meeting that challenge each day with excellence—and with dimples—how can WLW-Television lose?

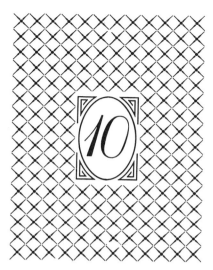

On November 6, 1967, Phil Donahue started the present *Phil Donahue Show* on WLWD, Dayton. The old roller rink, where WLWD now is, will never be the same again. And, for that matter, neither will the women who sit in daily with this intellectual imp of an Irishman. He understands women. They understand him. Phil Donahue, winner of the Golden Mike Award plus a first place citation from the National Association of Television Program Executives, though terribly successful, is still unsure of his success. He doesn't look upon himself as an entertainer. He considers himself a newsman of sorts.

His show, via tape, has appeared on many stations other than the ones that fly the Avco Television banner. It is seen in New York, Cleveland, Detroit, Philadelphia, Miami and cities all the way to San Diego. Sometimes it has been seen via tape—and therefore delayed. Other times it has been aired live in some of these distant cities to allow viewers there to telephone in and participate in the program, too.

One hesitates to call it a show because it isn't quite that. It is a program—and a good one.

Guests—invited ones on the platform with Phil and those in the studio audience—have been known to tangle head-on. Example: once the program endured a real live "sit-in." It was staged by Women's Liberation leader Robin Morgan and a group of her more militant followers. Miss Morgan, who was scheduled to debate *Playboy* executive Ansen Mount on the *Donahue Show*, arrived in Dayton the morning of the show. But once at the studio, in the preliminary get-together that Phil holds with his guests of the day, she got her back up and refused to go on. Her premise: she had been misinformed about the format of the program.

When the program that day opened, the program content itself was still up in the air, completely unresolved. Phil introduced Mr. Mount. But there was no Miss Morgan in the chair beside him. She and her band were seated on the floor in front of the set. Things started off in a touchy fashion and got touchier fast. When the *Playboy* representative began to speak, Miss Morgan mounted the stage, took the microphone away from Phil, and began to make *her* statement, too.

"I want to address my sisters who are watching the program," she announced. "The decision to stage this demonstration was made collectively. *Playboy* magazine makes million of dollars by making us sex objects. We have decided to take over this program and run it in our own way. We would like to invite our sisters to help liberate this situation. The men are not going to tell us what to do."

Actually, for the rest of that program everyone was telling everyone else what to do. Yells and shouts and polite smiles and frozen glares were the order of the day. Miss Morgan yelled at Mr. Mount. Callers—seething at home—called to yell at Miss Morgan. Liberationists in the studio audience yelled at the callers. And, actually, with everyone yelling at once, the program was like the final scene of *You Can't Take It With You.*

Mr. Mount trying to get words in edgewise, finally got to say, "I'm having a good time. Most talk shows are dull. *This* program is anything but dull. Besides, we at *Playboy* have the chance to express our philosophy to twenty million readers every month. I'm glad to give these women a chance here to express themselves."

When things quieted down—which was rare during that particular program—talk centered around a bunch of things: the role of the black woman in the Women's Liberation Movement, the role of the Playboy Bunny in society; the progress of equal employment, who-should-pick-up-whose-dirty-underwear—the-husband-or-the-wife—and who did Phil Donahue think he was. That day Phil wasn't too sure. He wasn't sure who anyone was. When he approached a lady in the studio audience with his microphone so that she might air a question or an opinion, he said, "Yes, sister? Do you want to ask a question?"

She glared back at him, then shouted emphatically, "I'm *not* a sister! I'm a happy housewife!"

Ladies—in the studio audience—cheered!

Another show in the can!

Some of his programs are less violent to air than others. But on any of them one thing is certain. There will be no small talk or idle chitchat. Idle conversations of little consequence turn Phil Donahue off fast, whether the conversations are held on the program or in a meeting with clients or at a social gathering of suburbanites. Small talk is not the stuff that Phil Donahue is made of.

"We have the hardest time," said Avco's Don Dahlman, "with conversations when setting up press conferences and interviews with Phil. At a press luncheon, if the talk turns to trivia, Phil just seems to withdraw into himself, pleasantly and not impolitely, but there he goes. He wants no part of talking about the weather. He is one of the most 'aware' persons I've ever met, but in some ways, the most 'unaware.' Trivia is not his way of life. It shows, too, on the program and that reluctance of his to make idle chitchat has made the program head and shoulders above all other talk shows . . ."

Everyone has appeared with him. Well, *most* everyone. For instance, seventeen-year-old Peggy Burt of Columbus, Ohio, shared her experiences as a hijacking victim in that Middle East hubbub of 1970 when the Popular Front for Palestine seemed to be the air traffic controllers for anything with wings and economy seats. Appearing with the young girl on the *Donahue Show* was Captain Grady B. Stone, Chairman of the Flight Security Committee for the Airline Pilots Association.

A poised and articulate Miss Burt, told how she spent the summer studying in Europe and was returning to New York on a Swiss Air flight when the plane was hijacked to Jordan. "A woman hijacker spoke over the loud speaker and said that she was from the Popular Front for Palestine and was the new captain of our airplane," said Miss Burt. "We were stunned and it took awhile for us to realize what was happening. We were not told where we were going but that our destination was a friendly country and the people would welcome us." But the passengers were not exactly welcomed with open arms when they reached Amman. "When we attempted to get off the plane they began shooting at us," she told the Donahue audience. "I think they were just shooting in the air to frighten us. But there were guerillas at all exits guarding us with guns while we were on the plane." During the course of the one-hour television show, she described her night in a bomb shelter, and recalled spending one night in the hall of a hotel. Asked what she had learned from the experience, she told Phil, "We must work for special change in a non-violent way. Now I have seen what violence can do. People can get so wrapped up in a 'cause' that they forget about human beings."

Are you beginning to get the idea? Phil Donahue's program—though aimed at the housewives—is no light frothy fare of flower arranging and who-said-what-to-whom-in-Hollywood. The program has come a long way since Phil faced his first guest back there in 1967. His first guest was atheist Madalyn Murray O'Hare—and that seemed to set the pace from there on. Others have trooped to Dayton to the ex-roller rink and to the show. To name a few: Bob Hope, Johnny Cash, George Wallace, Ralph Nader, Johnny Carson, Margaret Mead, Chet Huntley, Colonel Sanders, Jim Brown, Paul Lynde, and Art Linkletter. The format is simple. Each day Phil Donahue will have one guest or a group of guests with a common problem, such as *Playboy* staffer and the Women's Lib gal. "We try to keep the program simple and uncluttered," Phil himself explains. "There are no bands, no comics, no vocalists. We have the freedom and the flexibility of time. We have sixty minutes to delve into an issue and get to the heart of it."

[195]

Phil Donahue and his assorted guests have gone into just about everything. Some of the subjects tackled have been abortion, campus unrest, skyjacking, astrology, venereal disease, and heart transplants. Now and then a sexual turncoat will appear, transvestite or lesbian or whatever other delightful one-person combination is treading the boards that week. People phone in from home and Phil Donahue favors that. "The phone calls," he said, "are very important to us. It was a phone-caller who asked Tommy Smothers if he believed in God, and Bob Hope how much Chrysler spent on his Christmas Show. When the topic is terminal illness, we have calls from patients dying of cancer; when we discuss prostitution or drug addiction, we inevitably have calls from those who know what they are talking about. Women have shared marital problems with us over the telephone. College students have shared their concerns about society."

Willing to give anything a try, Phil Donahue has prepared soul food with Miss Black America, exercised with sexy take-it-off gal Gunilla Knutson, practiced witchcraft with Louise Huebner, modeled men's fashions for Oleg Cassini, joined others for an intensive sensitivity session, and climbed into bathtubs to demonstrate the newest ideas in home decorating. When a remote location is effective, Donahue and his crew troop to Art Linkletter's Beverly Hills penthouse, don bathing suits for a poolside interview, or journey to New York's Village Haven for Female Drug Addicts. As the result of Phil Donahue's Village Haven Show, the home received more than $8,000 in unsolicited contributions. Among Phil's favorite guests are Baroness Maria von Trapp (whose life story is told in *The Sound if Music*), because, says Phil, "Maria is a link between the old world and the new." When asked what she thought of youth in hippie garb, she replied without rancor, "They look like unmade beds." Another favorite guest for Phil is Dr. Benjamin Spock. Says Phil, "He takes criticism better than anyone I've ever met; and any millionaire who has made his mark and could be out fishing but devotes himself instead to something he believes in has to be admired, regardless of how you feel about his political views." Another favorite is Papa Leone, the Chef Extraordinaire, who carries his mother's picture with him when he visits the Donahue program and asks Phil to hang it on the set. People Phil would love to have as guests: Paul Newman, Muhammed Ali, Spiro Agnew, and Congresswoman Shirley Chisholm.

Says Phil himself, "I feel very lucky to be doing what I'm doing. How many people get the chance to spend a day with Al Capp, Edmund Muskie, or Dina Merrill? Sure, there are discouraging times, too. Sometimes I think, wouldn't it be nice to be an artist and to finish a painting and sit back and enjoy it? In this business, we may do a great show one day and get ready to pat ourselves on the back, but then we remember that there's tomorrow, and that next week's guest has just cancelled. We have 245 shows a year to produce. There are bound to be Jerry Rubin days." Phil admits the Jerry Rubin show was his longest hour! "What are we trying to prove? That a show like this can come from Dayton, Ohio, and that it can be a stopping-off place for important people who have something—we hope—important to say . . ."

Went up to Dayton one rainy summer morning to sit in with the Donahue show and see it from the inside out. Having spent too many years in advertising agencies where success is measured in terms of corner offices and the number of windows you have, I had to throw away this system of judgment because roller-rinks-turned-television-stations, especially of the Quonset hut variety, lack such attributes. WLWD, where the program originates, is located on the south side of Dayton in a commercial area surrounded by all sorts of stores, traffic patterns, and one-way streets none of which take you the direction you wish to go. I circled trying to get to WLWD and felt an even greater wonder for Phil Donahue. That women were in the studio audience each morning was a testament to his efforts. To get there, unless you're a native, isn't easy. But I digress. Point is, Phil Donahue has no corner office.

His office—really, a suite of small rooms each smaller than the other—is located on the second floor of the station. There is one office, beautifully and busily littered, where the secretary sits and where the visitors are greeted. Then, from there to the next office, you pass through a well-appointed sitting room no bigger than several broom closets. It is in the "sitting room" between the two offices that the guests for the day are parked, drink coffee, and talk with Phil before going downstairs a few minutes before 10:30 when the show itself starts. As I sipped coffee I thought about all the others who had been closeted in that little room with Phil. It made for pleasant and exciting thinking, associating in some vicarious way with people—*interesting* people—from all walks of life. I also had the uneasy feeling that if the place were still a roller rink I would have been where the many-mirrored globe would have been twirling suspended and glittering from the cavernous ceiling. I thought of that long-ago WLW time salesman, forever nameless, who used to unnerve the receptionists at advertising agencies by entering and saying with a blithe and worried voice, "When I was here last week, did I leave my skate key?"

He was also the one who insisted that lions and tigers do not roar. "The noise they make," he would tell anyone who would listen, "is really the animal clearing its throat." He would then proceed to demonstrate, clearing his throat with a roaring noise, loud enough to cause the others waiting in the reception area to look upon him with suspicion. He is no longer at WLW but whenever I hear a lion roar or visit a skating rink, I think fondly of him.

Anyway, there I sat, waiting for Phil, and there was Phil, looming in the doorway. He is, off camera, a cordial and soft-spoken man who has a faint aura of perpetual worry about him, like will the world last and will he measure up. I had met him earlier when he did his program in Columbus from the Ohio State Fair. He would try to move quickly from the stage to the trailer which was his office, but invariably ladies of every age would waylay him to talk. His memory was remarkable. One lady asked if he remembered when her daughter, a year before, had been one of those who telephoned in about this or that guest. He *remembered*. I thought at first he was putting her on, but he wasn't. He actually remembered. He recalled the daughter, the conversation, and the whole bit—with no prompting from the lady who queried him. I was, in some way, pleased. And from that moment on, seeing the real interest he expressed to that lady, I was in his corner for keeps. He wasn't Show Biz. He was real. The cameras had not lied to me.

So we sat in that office, drinking coffee and talking. Phil Donahue recognizes—sometimes with glee and sometimes with sadness—that the Donahue program is unique

[199]

unto itself. It is not a "talk" show in the format of Johnny Carson or Dick Cavett. Sometimes he wishes it were; sometimes he is glad that it is not. In his own quiet way, he and his staff are pioneering new television. Each week, via the guest list, they embark on an unknown exploration, hoping there will not be too many blind alleys in the offing.

"One of the biggest problems," he said, "is the guest. The real problem is, which one to turn down. We turn down many of them. We have to, Dick. Some of the guests who are booked on other talk shows and are winners are just not for us. I mean, a lot of people who can do a great eight minutes on the Johnny Carson Show aren't able to do an hour on ours. It's not their fault nor ours. It's just the nature of the show. But that is difficult for many people— agents and promoters and even viewers—to understand. They think a guest who is good enough to be with Douglas or Carson is certainly good enough for the Donahue program. But it doesn't follow. Not that we think we're better than those programs, but we have only one guest, and for a full hour, so we're married to that guest. That means that when we die, we die big. We're there an hour, no matter what, and there's nothing worse than a bad program for us."

This thought seemed to sadden him. He poured another round of coffee and said, "When someone comes up to us and says, 'Listen, I got a good show for you,' we say, 'Okay, but where is your guy going to be on? The Today show? We'd like to see him.' What I mean is, we seldom book a guest blind. We seldom book a guest on the enthusiasm of someone who saw him wearing lampshades at a party the night before. The real criterion, I guess, is will my wife watch him for an hour? That's pretty much the question we ask ourselves when considering a guest. In every city we're in, we are unashamedly beaming our program toward women. But this can be misunderstood, too."

True, true. Most programs offered milady are pap of little consequence. A few on Madison Avenue feel they have somehow *psyched* out the lady of the house. Her mainstay in life, they feel, is a toilet bowl neighbors will cluck over in admiration. These few forget that women are also people, capable of people-thoughts. There's more to life than a neighbor who mutters about the way your wash is—or isn't. Phil recognizes this. He is, in reality, friend to the friendless. He admires the brains these beauties have. He admires their thoughts as well as their sexuality.

"We have found," he said, really warming up, "that the traditional television fare for women is how to do covered dishes; what's new in floral arrangements; and tricks in home decoration. But listen, Dick, we have also found that women read more than the women's section of the newspaper. Women read more than their husbands do—most of them, that is. Many women hide the fact they are smarter than their husbands. And we've found that women converse in a more enthusiastic and interesting way than men do."

"Give me an example," I said.

"Men," he said, "talk *at* you. Women talk *with* you. Men pronounce. Women chat. If you're at a party, in the kitchen where the men are gathered and the women are gathered elsewhere, as seems to be our culture, listen to the different way the male and female conversations are carried out. In the women's group, one will say, 'I got hit by a truck this morning.' And the other women will say, 'You're kidding! Where? Are you all right?' Try the same opening, though, in the kitchen where the men are. I promise you that when someone says he got hit by a truck that morning, there will be at least one man in the group who will say, 'Yes, but wait till I tell you what happened to *me*.' Generally speaking, men don't listen to the responses to their own brilliant little speech. They're waiting and warming up for their next brilliant little speech. This has happened time and again on our program. We accommodate women mostly on the telephone for obvious reasons of the time of the day we are on the air but let a man get on the telphone and it's over. He has the answer. Period. It's a matter, I guess, of listening and not listening."

"Do you ever fall into that trap?"

He grinned. "You bet. It's easy to get trapped into *not* listening. Watch me on the program and you'll see. Suddenly, you're looking at the guest for the day, not hearing him, but wondering instead is the program making it. Anyway, I have a sort of inferiority complex about the program. When I look at the nighttime shows like *Laugh-In* with the cut, edited bits, and the musicals with all that lavish stuff, I see our program isn't really much. Those shows *move*. Then, I look at our program and I say what the hell are we doing? Our program is visually dull. We're there on one set, in a cage almost, with no band to save us, no pretty girls to break the monotony, and—well, listen, when we sit around here talking about these things, which we do, we get an awful insecure feeling. We also understand that the fact we are different may have provided us with some of the success. And I guess I really don't want to tamper with our present format. Still, I dream once in awhile. When Johnny Carson gets into trouble, he can cue the band. If

[202]

I'm in trouble, *I'm* in *trouble*. There's nobody I can cue anywhere."

"What was your most difficult program?"

Phil thought about that for a minute, looking even more worried.

"Leroy Jenkins," he said at last, "was a disaster. Religion, also, seems to provoke more mail than any other subject including sex. Any phase of religion, I mean. It used to hang me up but not too much anymore. I'm such a restless Catholic . . ." He stared at his empty cup a moment, then said quietly, "I think other programs miss the boat by not booking more theology discussions. Is there really a Hell? If God's so good, why is there a Hell in the first place? Does the fact that Jesus was white—or *was* Jesus white? These would be valid things to discuss. There seems to be a tremendous need to hang on to the absolute. There seems to be a tremendous need not to shake things, not to start fooling around with these absolute truths. But this was imposed on us while we were growing up. And now we're living in such an insecure world, it seems. If a guest comes on the program and starts fooling around with Jesus, some viewer simply won't tolerate it. Oh, I don't know. Generally, the whole business of youth defecting from the church fascinates me and I think it should be examined. Look around. Fewer and fewer young boys are in church on Sunday. Let's talk about it and see why. Let's get it out in the open."

But will Avco Broadcasting let him?

"Yes," he said. "They've given me an absolutely free hand. To be honest, there would be no way to do a show like this if there was not a mature management group letting it happen. If I had to worry about what the bosses were going to say after every show, I'd be a neurotic in two weeks. They've given me a free hand when sometimes I know it has probably hurt them. But they're more interested in good programming than the quick buck. Listen, in the history of this program everything has happened. Sponsors have cancelled. Angry letters have been sent to just about everybody in management. But throughout the whole experience not once have Mr. Murphy or Mr. Dahlman ever come to me and complained because I did something. I'm sure both of them have been tempted to do it many times, but they trust me. They know I'm not going to intentionally get anyone into trouble. But when you do upwards of a thousand programs—ranging from abortion to atheism and homosexuality, when you do shows that challenge the virtue of automobile manufacturers and breakfast-food makers, when you have guests like Nader and Lester Maddox and Ben Spock, somebody out there is going to get awful mad—and that somebody might just be a string-puller."

Letters *have* inundated Avco Broadcasting at times, filled with angry complaints aimed at the Phil Donahue program. These letters are not tossed aside. They are read, their contents digested, and the gripes are noted. Board members of the parent corporation have received letters that muttered, "Hey, do you know what's going on in Dayton. They had Jerry Rubin on that show! Do you want this country to cave in?" Such letters are received, digested, and noted.

"But," said Phil, his voice firm, his soul firm, "our view is that there are far too many people who want television to say only what they themselves like to hear. Some have decided that's the way to run this country. But we feel that the best way to insure the continuing vitality of rad-

[204]

icalism is to suppress it and so to give radicals more to gripe about. Suppression doesn't work. Bring these things out into the open and let the people see firsthand the Jerry Rubins. He is his own worst argument. If viewers would have our program removed because we had Jerry Rubin or a homosexual, I suggest the viewer look over all the guests for fifty-two weeks to get the total picture of our program. This show is not a parade of freaks. We ask those who complain about our sex shows to look over our schedule. They will see that such programs are less than seven percent of what we do. Listen, Dick, I could do a whole month of programs on lawns and garden, a different garden expert every day, and in the middle of that month put on Dr. David Reuben who wrote *Everything You Always Wanted to Know About Sex—But Were Afraid to Ask* and—I promise you—I'd get mail from viewers asking how come I'm always putting on sex. But we've had Dr. Norman Vincent Peale on our program. We've had the president of Notre Dame. Nobody writes in and complains about that. The only things they remember are the homosexuals and the lesbians and that was only one program out of 245! But we're proud of this variety. And we're determined not to permit the program to become one-dimensional by programming Jonathan Winters on Tuesday because we had a Vietnam debate on Monday.

"We actually *orchestrate* the program. We look, for example, at the middle of October and say, okay, we've got this kind of program Monday, what do we want Tuesday? Women's Lib is available Thursday. That being the case, do we really want an abortion show on Friday since abortions would be somewhat involved with the Thursday program. Do we want two subjects that closely related back-to-back? And, since the schedule might look heavy that particular week, one of us will always say, 'Okay, let's see if Tiny Tim is available!' I mean, I think it's important to be silly as well as serious. I think a little nonsense every now and then is treasured by the best of men. That's what my grandmother used to tell me and I believe it. If we put five senators on the program, five days running, by the time we had the fifth senator, we'd have nobody out there in TV land at all . . ."

By then the guests for the day arrived. Phil excused himself for a moment and left me in the little sitting room with a lady and gentleman who had apparently just flown in from New York. They had about them the look of exhausted travelers who had got up earlier than usual to catch a plane. While waiting for Phil to return, I made chitchat with them. The lady, it seemed, was tooting about the country selling legislatures on the merits of making abortions legal.

"How is it going?" I said.

"We're making progress," she said.

"Fine," I said, not knowing what else to say.

So I turned to the gentleman who had come in on the same flight and, I presumed, was with her in the venture.

"I think she may have a point, don't you?" I said.

All he did was glare at me.

Turned out he was traveling around the country fighting her stand.

We three waited, in stony silence, for the return of Phil. I could never, in a million years, get those two chatting again, but I had faith in Phil. I had absolute faith. And the program that rainy day was, by all standards, a huge success.

AND now, if we may, let us sing of Paul Dixon. "People who need people" so the song goes, "are the luckiest people in the world." This makes Paul Dixon extra lucky. He not only needs people, he needs *lots* of people! Audiences—studio audiences, that *is*—turn him on and the rest is midwestern magic. They *give* to him, he *gives* to them, and all the rest of us out there in WLW-Televisionland reap the benefit. To those who don't know what a *Paul Dixon* is, I say simply, sorry, but I don't think I can explain him to you. Those who *do* know what a *Paul Dixon* is need no explanation. A Paul Dixon is a Paul Dixon is a Paul Dixon is a Paul Dixon.

Right now, as I write this, Paul Dixon is that brash and wonderful and beautiful man who gets on the tube each morning at nine and holds forth until 10:30 doing—*what?* He sits behind a desk littered with gifts that that day's studio audience has presented him. The gifts are as brash and wonderful and beautiful as he is. Some of the ladies in his audience knit him nose-warmers. Others present him with comic greeting cards which, if they are clean enough (and some don't seem to be) he will read over the air and get the biggest kick out of. He is, one might suppose, the only comedian on television today whose staff of writers is lodged in Kansas City, working the funny side of Hall-mark. But on the other hand, he has no staff of writers. He has only himself, his girl associates (one day Colleen Sharp, the next Bonnie Lou), the prop men, the cameramen, the engineers in the booth, and the studio audience composed mostly of young chicks with nice knees which, of course, he admires each morning with binoculars. Simply put, that's his show. Add commercials and there you are. He has been doing it for ages now, he himself never ages, and —well, a Paul Dixon is a Paul Dixon is a Paul Dixon. Just don't ask for explanations. *Believe!* Everyone else does, including his sponsors.

Time was at WLW-Television when Ruth Lyons seemed to own the cash register. Now Paul Dixon seems to have inherited the golden touch. But *his* touch is not *her* touch and *their* touches are not Bob Braun's. Each of the three— Miss Lyons, Mr. Dixon, and Mr. Braun—are uniquely themselves. But Miss Lyons and Mr. Braun are sung of elsewhere in this volume. In this chapter, we sing of Mr. Dixon who doesn't sing too well himself but does so every chance he gets.

One morning I sat in the office of that most delightful Bill McCluskey, when gathering background for this book, and I never saw him so enthused which is an understate-ment because he gets enthused a lot. He waved a sheet of paper at me, could not contain himself at his desk, got up and came over in front of me, still waving the paper.

"Look at this," he said, fairly bubbling. "The next year is going to be the greatest year in the history of our live shows. I went down to Walt Bartlett's office before you came and I had to show him this—" again waving the paper. "This is the closest anybody around here has ever come to equaling what Ruth Lyons did. She had ninety commercial announcements a week, eighteen a day, and that was something! Well, Paul and Bob Braun both are now hitting eighty announcements a week. By fall, they'll hit ninety! That equals the Ruth Lyons record. Don't you see, Dick? Paul Dixon and Bob Braun are really something."

Yes, Bill McCluskey, I see, I see.....

As I sat there, pleased that Bill was pleased, I sensed that Miss Lyons would be pleased, too. Television, supposedly so fierce and so dog-eat-dog, is not always that way around the halls of WLW-Television. Ruth Lyons—and several others—have given WLW-Television a behind-the-scenes mood that few stations can duplicate. There is a sense of "family." That was how I knew that Miss Lyons would not be angry but would be pleased at Dixon's and Braun's success. And so would the guys in the control room. That's the way WLW-Television is. On the other hand, it is no Mecca. Tempers flare. Talent will forever be talent and rightly so. Each day they put their lives, their futures, and all their faults on the tube for all the world to see. This is bound to make talent at times hypersensitive. But, on the other hand, the tube has its own charm, too. If you are good, the tube will make you look better. If you are great—as Miss Lyons, Mr. Dixon, Mr. Braun, and Mr. Donahue are—the tube will do everything but deify you.

"Did you ever see anything like it?" McCluskey was asking, still bubbling. "Do you see, do you see?"

But do you, Bill McCluskey and all the rest, see that this chapter will be difficult for me as a writer to write? I can be objective as I write of Miss Lyons. I can be objective as I write of Mr. Donahue. But where Paul Dixon—and in some way Bob Braun—are concerned, my objectivity goes skittering out the window. The trouble is, I *know* Paul. And to make complete hash of my objectivity, I *like* Paul. I would like to believe that he and I are friends. So I can write of Paul here but know going in that I happen to be fond of the guy. I happen to think he's rather wonderful. So where shall I begin?

Oversimplified, Paul Dixon came from Iowa, worked a short while in Chicago radio, came to Cincinnati to be a newscaster ("the world's worst," said Mary Wood in the *Cincinnati Post & Times-Star* and in this judgment she bent over backwards to be kind because she happens to be fond of him, too), became a disc jockey ("Hi, Mom!") on WCPO, became a local television star—of sorts—when WCPO went into television (he pantomimed records with Dotty Mack and Wanda Lewis; and later, after Dotty got her own show, with Sis Camp), originated shows from here first for Dumont, then for ABC-TV; went to New York (causing the Dumont network to fold, causing ABC-TV to give up live shows in favor of flicks), and, at the request of WLW-Television's John Murphy, returned home again to Cincinnati where at first he did a lot of things on WLW-Television, one of them emceeing in part the *Midwestern Hayride.* Slowly his own show evolved, that was years ago, and there you are, but where are you?

Well, to the thousands and thousands of women—with

[210]

pretty knees—who have attended his morning show from the WLW-Television studios in Cincinnati where you *want* to be is in the front row of the studio audience so he can see what pretty knees you *do* have. That's how he got the title of The Mayor of Kneesville. Other than looking at knees and giving away sausages and doing commercials and letting Bonnie Lou or Colleen Sharp sing, that's his show—and we are right back where we started from. Sorry, Paul, I'll try again on another tack.

Years and years ago, when television was young (it aged: Paul Dixon has refused to), Paul used to do a pantomime show from the studios of WCPO-TV. This was when Dotty Mack, Wanda Lewis, and Sis Camp assisted with the chores. This was in the fifties, the early fifties and even the late-late forties, when television cables did not reach from New York to Cincinnati. What we got here were muddy kineoscopes of network shows, lots of men wrestling, baseball via the Cincinnati Reds, women roller-skating themselves silly, Ruth Lyons on WLWT, the *Midwestern Hayride* in its early video moments, Jim Stacey emceeing cowboy movies, Shirley Jester and Dick Hagemann wowing them on WKRC-TV, Willie Thall, and—well, there was Paul Dixon. No studio audience at WCPO-TV unless, that is, a delivery man wandered through. Paul pantomimed records, yacked up a storm, had fun, won friends and influenced sponsors, but however great he was in those days an ingredient was missing: ladies in the front row, howling over his antics. Cameramen don't laugh much and in those days they hardly laughed at all. To be Paul Dixon *then* was the same as trying to entertain the board of directors of a funeral home by wearing lampshades. Nonetheless, he had fun and the audience watching on the tube had fun.

But for the audience it was a snap. For Dixon it was work. *Hard work.* I suppose he might have given up the whole business of television and gone back into his old line of work, newscasting, but we all know what kind of a newscaster he was.

It was during this period I first met Paul. It was in the early fifties. I came to WCPO-TV first as a writer, then as a producer for the *Paul Dixon Show.* In those days of early television, Mort Watters who is one of the real geniuses of television, was batting about five hundred. For every Paul Dixon he hired—and got a winner—he hired a loser, too, like me, but in those days even to bat five hundred was to be already at genius-level. He hired me to "write" the *Paul Dixon Show,* then being fed for the first time to the networks. Well, I didn't write much, there was little that needed to be written, but in the time I was there, I got to know Paul Dixon well. He hasn't changed much except his hair style which I have a sneaking suspicion is not real. Paul then—and Paul now—was a guy wanting to please. He wants to please those in his present studio audience as he tried, back then, to please those of us in the control room. He wanted to please Mort Watters for whom he felt and still feels respect and gratitude for giving Paul his real start in front of the cameras. Today he wants to please John Murphy—and all the others in all the offices of Avco Broadcasting. He wanted and he wants to please those people out there watching him on the tube. He wanted and he wants to please those sponsors who shell out hard cash to advertise products on his show. And, in some lonely way, he has always wanted to please himself but because he is Paul Dixon he has never quite figured out how. I mean this seriously. Paul Dixon, I suggest, has tried so hard over the years and given so much of himself to please all those listed here (as well as his family) that when it comes to pleasing himself he is at loose ends and does not honestly know how.

"How did I do?"

He has asked me that question many times. In the old WCPO-TV studios on Symmes Street, Cincinnati, after the network show was completed; after the agency men had gone back to their hotels; after the sets had been struck; after the talent had scattered here, there, and everywhere; after the magic of the moment of telecast had dwindled into a stomach full of nagging doubts; I would come across him in his office, sitting alone, exhausted, and he would look up full of doubt and never-knowing, and ask,

"How did I do?"

Back then we used to do "remotes" from Coney Island. Paul Dixon would pack the park with fans, and those afternoons were hot and sweaty and wonderful. Only after the broadcast was over and the women who had come to see him were riding the ferris wheel and the engineers had gathered up the miles of coaxial cable and the last child had got the last autograph from him and there would be a moment—a brief respite of silence—he would look at me still full of doubt and never-knowing and ask,

"How did I do?"

Paul Dixon has not changed much over the years. So some people say. Our paths parted and, years later, when his morning program on WLW-Television was just beginning to gather steam, I visited Cincinnati and Dixon. After the show, we sat in his office (listen, he had a smaller one then; you should see the one he has now!) and we talked over "old times" and how well his WLW show was going and there was a lull in the conversation and he looked at me still with that doubt and never-knowing and he said,

"How did I do?"

Paul Dixon, after trying and succeeding in New York television, was glad to come back "home" to Cincinnati. He tells it best in his own book *Paul Baby*.

". . . In New York, John Murphy had dinner with Marge and me. We talked about many things—television and raising kids. Our Pam and John Murphy's daughter Pat had been friends before we had left for New York. When fathers have beautiful daughters, the conversation just naturally ain't all business! But after John left that evening, talk about being homesick! Marge and I loved New York, we don't put it down, but I guess we are just not the New York types. Certainly our kids weren't. Those two still thought our real home was back in Cincinnati—and that New York was only temporary. John Murphy's visit had brought everything into focus: New York was great, but the Dixons didn't want to live there . . .

"When I came back I did the same kind of show I had always done: record pantomime. The show was seen in Cincinnati, Dayton, and Columbus. I suppose the show was good enough. But something had happened to television, hadn't it? When television was new, a pantomime record show could capture the imaginations of viewers. But television had matured and our show hadn't. It was just creaking along, just doing pretty good—and no more. When John Murphy called me to his office, I was scared. I thought I was going to be given the sack. But I reckoned without John. I can still remember sitting in his office and feeling relief flood me as he explained his programming dream: a *live* morning show aimed at an *adult* audience.

He had tinkered with the dream with Mel Martin. Now he was dusting off that dream and asking me if I wanted to make it a reality.

" 'With a studio audience, Paul,' he said, 'And with a band. No records. What do you think?'

"I wasn't sure. My broadcast career till then had been with recorded music.

" 'Do you think I can do it?' I said finally.

"He nodded.

"And that was that!"

Understatement of the year—or decade. Because that was the start of the present-day *Paul Dixon Show* which does the same thing over and over again—differently— each and every day, five days a week. Bruce Brownfield and the band have been with Paul Dixon from the beginning. Bruce was around WLW even before then, though. *His* father, a musician, too, used to bring young Bruce around when he played on the *Ruth Lyons Show* . . or, to be technically correct, the *50/50 Club*. Bonnie Lou has been with Paul since the start of the program. Colleen Sharp has been added. And as for special guests—well, they are few and far between. The *Paul Dixon Show* has no need of guests. Its guests are the pretty ladies in the studio audience who daily "write" Paul Dixon's program via product endorsements, comments on Paul's wife, and other remarks that heard on any other program might border on the erotic.

It is possible, with no stretch of the imagination at all, to look upon Paul Dixon as a kind of one-man "industry." Certainly his efforts bring in the dollars to the WLW-Television coffers.

Says Bill McCluskey, "Paul Dixon has many of the attributes that Ruth Lyons had. When a new product comes into the market and gets on the Paul Dixon Show, the stores just have to stock it. Grocery chains are aware of Dixon's selling power. There is a term in business: 'forced distribution.' That means a store will be forced at times to stock a product even though it has not wanted to. Dixon 'forces' distribution and advertising agencies and potential sponsors know it. When anyone wants to sell products to the housewives in the WLW marketing area, the first salesman they try for is Dixon. He can sell anything—and that's a fact."

But Paul Dixon is not the polished announcer with the golden tonsils. He makes hash of the best commercial copy ever written. The result of the hash he makes is a better commercial, one that only Dixon could do (or get away with), and the commercial *sells*. While he can read lines, he is not very good at it. I speak from experience. I used to write for him.

But this is his charm, don't you see? Like Arthur Godfrey he is *himself*. He is the guy next door, if you live in that kind of a neighborhood. He is, in his own way, something rather special.

Besides, what other grown man do you know can walk down the street and have other grown men shout, "Hi, Paul Baby!" at him? Paul explains that phenomenon:

"The phrase," he says, "didn't originate with me because nothing on the show originates with me. I just arrive at the studio each morning and let the show happen. The phrase 'Paul Baby' originated with one of our prop boys, Al Bischoff, now with the Drackett Company. It's amazing how our prop boys have gone onward and upward to big things in the world. Most of them, when they are prop boys, are students at the University of Cincinnati or Xavier University. The irregular hours of their class schedules coincide with the irregular hours here at Avco Broadcasting, but none of this explains how I got the name 'Paul Baby,' does it? Well, a few years back I bellowed for the prop boy to bring me something from off camera. Al Bischoff handed it to me, leaned over, patted me on the head, and said cheerfully, 'Okay, Paul *Baby!*' And that was how that got started. The name has stuck with me ever since. I could never get rid of it, even if I wanted to."

Any chance of Paul Dixon going coast-to-coast on the networks? Not likely, says Bill McCluskey. "We tried syndication, too," says the amiable dancer of the Irish jig, "but it just didn't pan out. We all tried to make it work, but it didn't. We used the syndication format where the show stops every so often for local stations to run their local advertising—and that was what hung us up. There Paul would be, gabbing with a lady in the studio audience, 'getting rolling' as he would say, and everything would have to stop so the local stations could cut away for the local advertising. This would happen several times an hour. By the time the local stations would return to the Paul Dixon Show, the momentum that Paul Dixon had established would have evaporated. This stop-and-go kind of program got Paul, and everybody connected with his show, nervous. So we gave up the syndication idea, turned Paul and the gang loose for ninety minutes with no breakaway—and Paul blossomed again. I suggest that when you get a great format, you may tinker with it, but you know when to go back to the tried-and-the-tested. You can't be more tried and tested and effective than Paul Dixon."

Still, Paul worries. Check with him before the program

starts at nine each morning and you'll see him nervous as a cat. He is, by his own admission, nervous right up until the time he walks out in front of the studio audience. Then, magic happens. The butterflies go away and he is himself again. Dixon said it best in his book when he wrote:

"You crush out your cigarette, straighten your shoulders, and go—almost at a trot—onto that stage. The noise of the audience pours over you like warm water. You mug. They react. They laugh. You laugh. And the butterflies? What butterflies, lady? You're home again—among friends. And you proceed to do the same show you do every day. It's as simple as that."

The same show, but not *quite*, Paul.

Though those who watch are quick to admit that his show doesn't change from one day to the next—one lady, absent a year from WLW-Televisionland returned and found she hadn't missed a thing—the show nonetheless has evolved from a rather nervous production to the slick production it is these days. Gone from the program are the promotion gimmicks and the little contests usually found cluttering up most such shows when they begin. In fact, gone are most of the gimmicks. If there are any contests, they are the sponsors'. The station doesn't have to use tricks to get an audience for Dixon. He himself is tricky enough.

"I will not," says Paul in a quiet moment, "get too serious on the show. The purpose of the show is not to change the world. It is to entertain the housewives—those beautiful ladies!—for ninety minutes. Phil Donahue appeals to the intelligence of the housewives and in our way, we do, too. But his is the serious approach. Ours is the kidding approach. But there have been serious moments on our show, very serious moments."

Yes, Paul, and the good ladies out there have shared them with you.

The death of Bonnie's first husband.

The death of Greg, your son.

And your own particular moments when you lay ill in the hospital.

And so many more behind-the-scene lonelinesses.

But just as Red Skelton doesn't quit, neither does Paul Dixon. Both are clowns. Both are comedians. And both tend to look somewhat alike, especially when Paul is doing his "In The Book" routine, one of the few he brought over from the days of pantomiming. That routine, by the way, was created by Len Goorian, now manager of the Shubert Theater in Cincinnati, but back then a New York transplant, teaching Dixon the joys of dining out at Izzy Kadetz's Kosher Restaurant as well as teaching Dixon to tap dance. Dixon learned the first, never the second, but that's . all right. He doesn't sing too well, either.

To be a Paul Dixon—ninety minutes a day in everyone's home—is never to be able to sneak into a restaurant with Marge for a quiet dinner. Dixon's face is as familiar to all as the outline of Mount Adams or the shape of Cincinnati's new stadium down by the river. True, being Paul Dixon in a resturant means you get better service, but it also means you have little chance to eat whatever you have been served.

One night, Paul, Marge, and I were sitting in a little country restaurant in Butler County, Ohio. The place was deserted except for us, the waitress, the chef, and the owner.

We ordered. Marge and I got to eat. In fact, we were sitting around waiting for the dessert dishes to be cleared and poor Paul had yet to tackle his salad. When the waitress wasn't telling him how she watched him every day, the chef was telling him the same, and when neither was doing that, the owner—impressed with the fact Paul Dixon was eating in his establishment—sat beside Paul, close as he could get, bending his ear about how the restaurant would someday be redecorated. Paul sat through this good-naturedly. And, before leaving, he managed to get a bite of his salad. But outside in the parking lot he sighed and said:

"Dick, can you see why I eat home a lot?"

Marge just stood there, grinning.

Wonderful girl, that Marge. On the air, of course, Dixon bemoans her activities and her rich tastes and her free-handedness with credit cards. He says, on the air, that she makes him sleep in the basement. Women, meeting Marge on the street, bawl her out because of this. Men have, too. Marge says nothing. Just stands there, grinning. She's okay, and Paul knows it. They have come a long way together from the days they dated when they were grade school kids in Iowa. They have come a long way but have not changed. New York didn't change them. Chicago didn't change them. All the exposure Dixon has had in this area—and elsewhere—has not changed them. This, in fact, is the charm of Dixon on the air. He is himself. And who he is, is real. Phonies don't last on the tube. You have to be real to stick around as long as a Paul Dixon. Very, very real. Does he sleep in the basement? Does Marge make him cover up her petunia at the first sign of frost? Did those chickens *really* get married?

Does it really matter?

Humility. That seems to be Paul Dixon's underlying force. He doesn't *seem* humble, of course, when seated at the desk telling some nice lady in the studio audience to shut up. But he says it with a grin—and she understands because she knows that he is gabby, too. But look at the show carefully. Humility *is* there. Paul Dixon plays second banana—as they say in show business—to everybody there. He's the straight man for the members of the band, whichever girl is there that day, the prop boys, the cameramen, the ladies in the audience, and—upon occasion—the props, most of which he never seems to master. His clumsiness is so perfected one would think he was a true master at it. He isn't though. When he appears clumsy on camera he isn't kidding. You should see him off camera. But throughout the ninety minutes of the show—and the rest of his working day—Paul Dixon listens and tries to learn, never believing that he is quite good enough. He listens to advertising copy writers fresh out of college, the shoeshine man, John Murphy, Bill McCluskey, strangers who stray into his office, and, when he goes out to lunch, to the cab driver, waiter, and the fat lady who stopped him on the street to tell him how she liked—or didn't like—his show. By the time he gets home at night, he is listened out.

I remember many moments with Paul Dixon. I remember him changing his shirt after each show. Each show, in some lonely way, exhausts him these days (the audiences never see this side of him), and he returns to his office, drenched. His fresh shirt is waiting there, in his attaché case. I remember him poring over his mail, letter after letter, gathering sustenance from the letters—some typed, some scribbled with pencil, some written with the shaky quaky hand of someone's grandmother. I remember him

[221]

sleeping in the back of a car as the car drives him to this or that appearance. I remember him sitting quietly, talking of his dog. I remember him once in a restaurant where he and I sat alone at the table, the mood was quiet, and the afternoon was waning, but Paul sat there exhausted.

"Live one day at a time," he said, his voice low and so serious. "I guess that's all any of us can do, Dick. I go on the show, do it, have fun doing it, but when it's over. . ."

He made a helpless motion.

This is the Paul Dixon you never see.

He's too big a guy to let you see.

After a long silence, he looked up at me and said:

"You saw the show today, Dick. How did I do?"

I said nothing.

I mean, what can you say to a friend you love? How can you tell him he's good. For one thing, he won't believe you. He does not believe that of himself. Since Iowa, since he was the hick town kid of the hick town druggist, Paul Dixon has been running real fast, grabbing for the brass ring, hoping for success. He has acquired brass rings by the dozens but he is not aware of it. He has had thus far, with much waiting in the wings, more success in this business of broadcasting than any ten men I know. But he doesn't believe it.

So there I sat, saying nothing. How could I say to him, "Listen, Paul, because of you dozens of people have jobs on your show and they don't have to worry about the fickleness of this business because you've built your show solid and it will last. Because of you, small businesses introducing products have grown into big businesses—and hundreds of guys in hundreds of factories have jobs because you're out there, selling what they make. Because of you and the dollars your show brings in, WLW-Television can afford to do public service shows that it never could have considered otherwise."

Yes, I could have gone on and on, but he wouldn't have believed me. So pretty soon we parted. He went one way and I went another. As I watched him walk, alone, down Sixth Street, headed back to the station, head down, tired, perhaps the loneliest man in the world right then, I could hear him say, in my imagination, "How did I do? How did I do?"

I didn't answer you then, Paul. But I'll answer you here.

You did fine.

You did just fine.

TWILIGHT—from John Murphy's office sixteen floors up in the Provident Tower—presents window-gazing that gives you mixed emotions. Down there—'way down there— used to be the red brick complex of Cincinnati's old waterfront. Now the Third Street Distributor dominates. The red brick buildings had been bulldozed away into yesterday. There is the stadium. There is the Ohio River. And over there, across the river, the minuscule towns of Covington and Newport, appearing to be mere toy towns, but they are not. The expressway traffic in the twilight rush hour of winter is frantic, like angry bubbles in a straw.

John Murphy sat at his desk, putting the finishing touches on the day, signing letters, gathering notes, but he still had another meeting to attend. It would be late before he himself joined the expressway crowd and tooted homeward.

We were saying goodbye. The book, for better or for worse, was for the most part completed and my adventure with WLW was nearing an end. I stood at the window and looked down at the rush hour traffic. Then I was aware that John Murphy was standing beside me.

"The stadium changes the whole picture of Cincinnati, doesn't it?" he said.

It does. It is no longer the Cincinnati of WLW's childhood.

Many factors make a city great. One of those factors is media: the voices of the community that come at you from the printed page, the picture tube, and the radio. Only the week before I had sat beside Francis Dale of the *Enquirer*, while he explained to me the beauties of the stadium we were then in.

I felt as I stood beside John Murphy at the window as I had felt that day in the stadium: that I was in the presence of giants. I do not mean this in the sense they must be flattered but in the sense such men are the *doers* of this community we call Greater Cincinnati. To stand beside the man whose energies and dreams helped make much of Cincinnati's—and the nation's—television come true is a beautiful moment that I will remember well.

To be a writer is to be lucky: to be a writer is to meet and know, for one brief moment, people who make the world happen. John Murphy was in a mellow mood at that moment and so was I. The end of a book always saddens me. I must say goodbye to so many people because others to be written about are waiting in the wings.

"What of the future?" I said to John Murphy.

He shrugged.

"Pay television," he said, "was supposed to swallow free television. But along comes cartridge television—and it's a whole new ball game. Who knows what twenty-five years will bring?"

"But Avco Broadcasting?"

"We'll be up front," said John Murphy. "We've got the product, we've got good men out on the street selling it, and we've got good management control. Programs and talents are the key. If you haven't got programs and talent, you might as well forget it. But we've got them."

"Your biggest problem now?"

He watched the cars stream by.

"Our biggest one at the moment is inflation," he said. "But we're not alone in that, are we?"

"What will your grandchildren see when they tune in WLW?"

He smiled.

"A lot of what we see now, but a lot more, too," he said. "Think of the things we were exposed to in the sixties, things like the moon landing. I think that as science develops, communication will develop, too. You'll still have 'live' television, but on a kind of combination basis. For example, if you walk into the average home today, you'll find shelves of books: the standards, the classics, the how-to-do-it books. The exact same thing will be there in the future, but instead of books, there will be television cassettes. It's exciting to think about, isn't it, and it isn't even here yet."

"In this business," I said, "you deal with all sorts of hypersensitive people. How can you keep from becoming hypersensitive yourself and blowing the whole bit?"

He shrugged.

"Sometimes," he said, "you just have to luck out. But

[227]

mostly, you have to stay with what's going on and watch it from all sides. Whether the plan is yours or not, you have to see if there are any weaknesses in the plan, and you have to correct those weaknesses."

WLW is more than a picture that flickers and talks and sings at you.

John Murphy, who had been silent for a moment, said with a sigh, "Do you know one problem, Dick? Everybody and his brother is a program director. Everytime I play golf, someone corners me to ask why we did that or that or why don't we do something else. It really gets to me after awhile."

"How do you get away from it?"

"I can't. But I try to control the situation. If I were a doctor, I'd run into the same thing, I suppose. A doctor goes to a party and in no time at all someone has him cornered, telling him the aches and pains. I know a lot of doctors and enjoy playing golf with them. They don't tell me what they don't like on television and I keep my aches and pains to myself. I guess the secret is riding with the punches. But I'm human, too. I went to this one party to relax after I'd worked a rough week but in ten minutes some guy had captured me and was telling me all the problems with the broadcasting. In an offensive manner, too. I just couldn't take it. Finally I said, I don't know about you but I want to relax and meet some nice people, do you mind? I walked away from him and got a drink. I suppose it wasn't right, but there are times you just have to do it or go home—or punch the guy in the mouth."

"Can you do as doctors do? Unplug your phone and not be home?"

"Nope," he said. "We've got a rule around here. Everybody has to be able to be found twenty-four hours a day, 365 days a year, and that includes me. You never know what's going to happen. We could be standing here, the phone could ring, and some high national official has dropped dead . . ."

When Paul Dixon had his heart attack, John Murphy was at the Heritage Restaurant about to eat. He didn't get a chance to eat until the next day.

We watched the lights wink on at the stadium. Darkness was filling the city. The expressway was still crowded. But my mind went back to Crosley Field when color television was just starting and to colorcast a night game was considered impractical and farfetched. My mind went back there because I was standing beside the man who made colorcasting of night games a reality. A corporation leader does more than sit behind a desk, push buttons, sign memos, and eat expensive lunches. Mr. Murphy had told me the story of color and night games . . .

"My father," he said, "used to make me recite every night —in addition to my prayers—that thing about 'building a better mousetrap' and I guess this has always impressed me. I mean, if you are not born into a well-to-do family— and I certainly wasn't—you still could be successful in this country if you worked hard, let your imagination develop, made that imagination work for you. Well, we were televising baseball in black and white but I was convinced that the addition of color would provide the one dimension that was lacking. But color was expensive. Not many color sets were around them. We did the Ruth Lyons show in color and sold many sets. But we had this great audience in baseball—and they weren't getting color. So I suggested to Bob Dunville that I head to New York and to RCA

[229]

and ask for a subsidy to put together a promotion selling color sets, deals with local distributors, things like that. There's more to television than putting on programs. Bob said I was going to have a sore fanny after being bounced down fifty-four floors of the RCA Building. I said, 'But isn't there also the chance RCA will say yes?' Well, I went to New York, made my presentation, and they *did* say yes. The plan worked so well, selling so many color sets, that RCA called the Cincinnati area 'Colortown USA,' and used our promotion elsewhere.

"But it wasn't as simple as it sounds. In the first New York discussions they asked if we had done any experiments in Cincinnati, trying to colorcast night games. They said they had done experiments—with light meters. I told them we were doing it with actual equipment. But I had to confess our success till then had not been good. But I told them we were convinced night games could be aired in color and that we would stay in touch, keeping them informed of our progress. If we were lucky, I said, I would return to New York with a videotape—in color— of a night game. Well, luck *was* with us . . ."

Luck? But I can't consider luck happening unless it's made to happen. I didn't tell John Murphy this, but I knew some of the story. Howard Lepple, an Avco vice president on the engineering side, just "happened" to meet up with a General Electric man who just "happened" to remember a tube that had been developed for the military, then not used. Avco Broadcasting just "happened" to test this tube, it changed night to day insofar as colorcasting games went—and New York was pleasantly surprised at what has been termed "a major breakthrough in the progress of television," a breakthrough that Avco Broadcasting made happen. Now, of course, colorcasting of night games is accepted as ordinary. But it was John Murphy and such men as Lepple who made the "ordinary" happen. Luck, imagination, persuasiveness—all of that went together. Luck alone had nothing to do with it. As the result of Avco Broadcasting's educated tinkering, a new world of color television opened for Cincinnati—and everywhere in the world television was. For the first time settings considered impossible to light for colorcasting could be lighted. Not only the fans of baseball benefited. So did basketball and football and hockey fans. And so did shut-ins, unable to attend special church services. They are now there—in color. Years ago, Powel Crosley's tinkering made the world of radio better. Today Avco Broadcasting's same thoughtful tinkering makes the world of television better—and, as we say, not just here but everywhere in the world. WLW is still leading the way. Let us give credit, then, where credit is due. Okay?

But before you think I'm trying to deify John Murphy and the WLW crew, let me toss another story at you. This can be considered Mr. Murphy's most painful moment. There he was, fresh out of New York, putting WLWD on the air in Dayton, and he went out and sold a department store on buying television. Everything was set up, a remote telecast had been planned for the store, Murphy and store officials were sitting in front of the set, waiting for the grand moment when—kerplunk! The picture faded and the remote bombed. Recalled John Murphy, "That remote had been promoted far and wide. Everybody who had a TV set in Dayton was waiting for this unusual (for then) experiment in remote telecasting. When the picture disappeared, I just sat there, but I

[231]

really wanted to crawl into the wastebasket and disappear . . ." This was in 1949. It doesn't seem like almost a quarter-century ago, does it?

I watched as John went about his office, turning off the lights.

An accessible man—almost too much so. "I've been criticized from time to time," he had told me once, "because I make myself *too* available. Lately, though, I'm becoming a little more careful about strangers coming in. I want to know first what they want to talk about. I hate to be that way, but there is so little time in the day these days. On the other hand, I take an awful lot of telephone calls . . ."

And grief—from viewers, listeners, talent, engineering, sales, and whoever else has a dime and John's phone number.

By the time we reached street level, the darkness of the city was complete: street lights were on, store windows glowed, and the nightly rush hour had evaporated. We parted company at Fourth and Vine: he going to his car and I to mine—and the book was over. I stopped into Izzy Kadetz's to say hello, he shouted hello and a bunch of other things, because some things never change. Certainly his kosher restaurant doesn't. On one corner: WLW. On another: Izzy's. The third corner at Ninth and Elm is occupied by Jack Abrams's saloon which Dixon calls the Mission. On the fourth corner are the drug store and WLW's radio facility. The night streets were deserted. A few lingerers were in the Mission, staring into their glasses. The steam from Izzy's steam table clouded his restaurant window. The drug store, lighted, seemed empty of everything but clerks. The WLW buildings—like fortresses—stood. But it was over, wasn't it?

[232]

As a boy in grade school I used to listen with a sense of wonder to the voices that came out of my radio. Back then, radio announcers seemed gods to me. But the gods have somehow diminished and become real. WLW has, in some sense, diminished from the lofty state that I imagined, and has become real, too. The voices of the people on radio and the people projected on my tubes are no longer strangers. We have become friends. When we pass on the street we speak, chat about our children, and the meetings—however delightful—are most ordinary. In growing old I am aware that Graham McNamee and Harry Von Zell and Norman Brokenshire and Peter Grant have been reduced in my heart to mortal status. I regret the passing of the gods.

I stood there, in front of the Mission, looking across the street at WLW, and felt melancholy. Then I watched as two ragmuffin lads—ten or eleven or twelve years old—wandered along Ninth Street to pause at the stone steps leading into the station. They stopped and stood. To be sure, they could have climbed the steps and gone into the station, but they didn't. They stood at the bottom of the steps, watching. Watching for what? An announcer to come out, perhaps, or a weatherman. Watching for a familiar face that had come into their homes via the tube. How long they waited, I don't know. I got in my car and left. But I felt better. For them the magic still held. That was good enough for me.

The gods are still the gods. It is only us worshippers who have been replaced.

Put that on your bumper sticker:

WLW LIVES!

INDEX

[235]